Rambling Through
Pleasant Memories

Tony Kinton

Rambling Through Pleasant Memories

Also by Tony Kinton:

www.tonykinton.com

Rambling Through Pleasant Memories

Tony Kinton

Cedar Arrow
PUBLISHING

Cedar Arrow Publishing
Copyright © 2013 – Tony Kinton

Cedar Arrow Publishing
books may be ordered through
booksellers or by contacting:

Cedar Arrow Publishing
Tony Kinton
P.O. Box 88
Carthage, MS 39051
www.tonykinton.com

Sherry Thornton's photography can be viewed and ordered by visiting: www.photographyonthewildside.com

Scripture taken from the King James and New International Version of the Bible.

ISBN: 978-0-9836829-1-2
Library of Congress Control Number: 2013908293

Printed in the United States of America

ACKNOWLEDGMENTS

For more years than I care to count, I have been privileged to write for a long list of publications. Many of these writings have revealed my strong proclivity for things old. Seems I was born 200 years too late! Still, many readers have been kind and have expressed a fondness for the old days and old ways about which I often opine. To date, some 2,000 of my varied articles have been published. And that brings me to those who, like the readers, were kind. They were kind enough to give me an opportunity to find my words in print. They were kind enough to allow me the freedom to put into their pages pretty much whatever I wanted to put there. And they have been kind enough to allow me to reprint many works previously published by them. Some of the writings in this book first saw printed life in some of those publishers' and editors' publications. I owe these publishers and editors a deep debt of gratitude.

To begin naming these individuals and their printed offerings opens me to criticism, for I can easily omit one or more in error. But I must. I am obligated to list some, at least those who were highly significant in my journey. There are the following: Mississippi Outdoors; Mississippi Sportsman; Mississippi Game & Fish, North American Whitetail, and Whitetail Journal, these publications of Game & Fish Publications; Cabela's Outfitter Journal; Bowhunter; Outdoor Life; Petersen's Hunting; Blackpowder Hunting; and Mossy Oak's Hunting the Country. All have been a positive influence in my life and career.

But I must now move to a duet of publications that hold a particularly warm spot in my heart. The deadlines for copy in these two are a time of excitement, for I enjoy every word I write in them. They are Today in Mississippi, the monthly publication produced by the Electric Power Associations of Mississippi. Debbie Stringer, editor, and the staff there are extraordinarily helpful and gracious. You, all of you, have my sincere appreciation.

And there is Primitive Archer magazine, the most fascinating publication with which I have been associated. Several years back the folks there allowed me to become hunting editor and this has been a high point in my life. Monroe Luther, Mike Moore, Ed Ingold and Marie Luther, to borrow a tired but valid proclamation, are the real deal. I am honored to find my name on the masthead of Primitive Archer. And if you have never read this fine magazine, you simply must. Pick up a copy at practically any newsstand and/or visit the publication's website: www.primitivearcher.com. Either route you take in digesting the information provided will be an intriguing adventure.

I must certainly offer my thanks to Sherry Thornton. While not a publisher, Sherry is a talented photographer. Her images have illustrated a great many of my articles, and one decorates the cover of the book you are now reading. Be sure to check out her work at www.photographyonthewildside.com. You will not regret the time spent there.

And please follow me on my website as well. I will try to keep it updated and interesting: www.tonykinton.com.

Thank you for taking the time to read my ramblings contained within these pages. I hope they inspire and relax you.

Contents

Memories From the Past; Lessons for the Future

As many of you, I grew up in an era far different from today. Technology as we now know it simply did not exist, and leisure time was no common commodity. Work was a constant. Most of this was on a poor-dirt country farm as we and hundreds like us attempted to scratch out a living in a hillside cotton patch, corn field, and garden spot. There were always a few cows about, and a pen containing meat hogs was standard. Employment outside the farm for anyone without professional training was hard to find.

But life was good. That statement may come as a surprise to those not acquainted with the situation mentioned above. I fear that we too often judge life today by possessions and how much work we can avoid. The good life of our modern society appears to focus on the exotic rather than the mundane. That, I suppose, is simply a sign of the times. Still, I hold to the words that open this paragraph: Life was indeed good. We had ample food, we were a close family, we knew and cared for our neighbors, we had peace and security, and we were happy.

When considering that life of earlier years, I am flooded with memories. Some are painful, such as when we lost a neighbor-hood friend or uncle or grandparent or a trusted pet. But more of those memories are joyous. Even riding from the field in a wagon loaded with sun-softened cotton after a hard day created memories of great pleasure. Nothing compares to the feel and smell of freshly picked cotton. But if I were forced to choose, I would have to say that the best memories came from times we spent in the woods and on the waters, sometimes all four of us and sometimes just my dad and me. These not only gave me a solid start as an outdoorsman and ultimately a writer spinning yarns about such adventures; these also gave me the opportunity to learn lessons about life that would be invaluable as I aged.

My dad was a dedicated squirrel hunter. Every Saturday morning during the season found the two of us in the woods along the Pearl River near home. He knew those woods and passed that knowledge on to me. Later, when I was in my last two or three years of high school, we branched out to a block of woods then known as the Forks of Tuscolameta. These, as did those of our initial ramblings, lay hard against the Pearl in some spots, but they were several miles removed from that tract near home that was so familiar. This unfamiliarity caused the Forks to seem far away, adventurous.

Squirrel hunting for us was a recreational pursuit, to be sure, but it meant a great deal more. For one thing, we ate every squirrel we took. Waste was never a consideration, and I was instructed to take a squirrel cleanly and swiftly. I learned from this, sometimes from verbal coaching and sometimes by simple example that all life is important and should be held in high regard. I learned that we are to use wisely what we have been given and we never take simply to be taking, never take simply to have more.

We didn't have a map of the Forks – if any existed then – and often we would come up on an old fence or slash of paint on a tree. Regardless of how tempting the squirrel timber looked over there, my dad would say, "I don't know. That may not be on company land." Although no one would have been the wiser, he would turn and stay clear of that property. The lesson, hardly ever verbalized, was to respect the rights and wishes of others. I came to realize, somewhat subtly I suppose, that integrity is not limited to those times when someone is watching.

Often during my earliest years in the woods, we would encounter a briar tangle or muddy slough. Dad would pick me up and carry me through. As I grew older, however, he would allow me to navigate such obstacles myself. Dealing with my difficulties was his responsibility when I was too young and inexperienced to do so, but when I became capable of taking care of myself the responsibility shifted. Not a bad lesson for living life.

And we fished during those formative years. The most memorable trips were when all four of us – dad, mom, my sister, and me – went to a lake in the Delta to catch bluegills. Mom always cooked breakfast on the bank near a favorite rock pile after a morning of fishing, and when we left that spot only ashes of the fire and footprints remained. No trash. And we never infringed on another angler. If someone was in a productive spot ahead of us, we went somewhere else. To do otherwise would have been disrespectful.

We don't hunt and fish together anymore. Years have, naturally, impeded that possibility to a significant degree. But the recall of those days when we did is still fresh in my mind. And the lessons are deeply ingrained, assisting me daily in interactions with others. These lessons were learned on the water and in the woods – not a bad classroom in my opinion.

I was never fortunate to have children of my own, but I do have one great nephew who is old enough to go and show a keen interest in the out-of-doors. I have begun taking him fishing and hunting. I hope to take those same lessons I learned and pass them on, for they are as significant today as they were in my childhood – these lessons from the past and for the future.

What Is It?

So what is it that makes a hunter a hunter? What burns deep within that coaxes us to the woods, the fields, the streams? What seemingly misplaced sentiment exists that would lead us to conclude that a tent in a secluded mountain meadow is more desirable than some luxuriously appointed setting tucked in tightly among others of its kind and filled with the trappings that much of modern humanity accepts as necessary? There may be no answer, or at least not one single answer. The entire concept is far too broad, encompassing far too many individuals and far too many persuasions.

It could be the way we were brought up. Some of us, and I am among that group, grew up hunting. For my family, hunting was not only a respite from the mundane of simple farm labor; it was a means, a method of subsistence. We hunted so that our menu would be supplemented. The norm of homegrown vegetables, canned fruit and domesticated pork, while more than adequate and always appreciated, often became tiresome. Hunting provided an avenue through which we could add to that ration squirrels, rabbits, ducks, and quail. There were no deer within the area back then. And as a result, hunting became a routine ingredient in my young life. It remained such as I moved into adulthood; it remains the same now as I enter those golden years.

Or it could be that we are hunters simply because of those modern trappings mentioned earlier. Hunting offers the opportunity to leave all that behind for a brief time, the opportunity to reconnect with something that is lost in the everyday for most of us. That is justification enough. And the collecting of game may be a minor character in the drama. Sought and appreciated, but not essential to the enjoyment, the renewing of spirit.

It certainly could be the rattle of aspens on an autumn breeze. It could be, as here in the Southeast U.S., that withered sweet gum leaf and its magical chatter as it lets go and drifts downward, bumping its likewise withered neighbors that remain stubbornly united with the stem that grew them last spring. It could be the yellows and browns and reds of the hickory or oak or poplar as summer looses its grip and fall brings relief from smothering heat. It could be the gentle gurgle of a diminutive stream trickling through rocks and timber, those same leaves of the aspen, sweet gum, hickory, oak or poplar decorating its surface and speaking silently of change.

It could be a first snowfall in the high country. It could be the cry of geese headed south. It could be a sleek whitetail doe tipping through hardwoods or a dainty pronghorn darting about the prairie or a bull elk bugling from a mountainside meadow. It could be Africa's grey ghost, his double-hexis headgear glistening amongst the thornbush. It could be the roar of a stag in the Scottish Highlands.

It could be any of or all these things. It could be more. But whatever that it is, it contributes to our proclivity as hunters. We recognize it to varying degrees, but we are no less lured by it even if we can't thoroughly isolate it, give it a name, point to it as the it. And it is powerful, resourceful, deeply entrenched. It quickens us. It is why we are hunters.

Tents: Structures Good for the Spirit

I always sleep best in a tent. Few there are, or so it seems, who share this possibly misplaced enthusiasm, but for me there has never been any question. I always sleep best in a tent.

Why that is so I cannot say. In fact, I am not completely sure. Perhaps the reason trails back to some Bedouin spirit of being mobile or some Bohemian propensity to be something or someone who shuns conformity. Could be, but these traits appear a bit radical for me. You see, I am fully domesticated in most of life. But there remains a strong urging that places me in a tent many nights in any given year. Not as often as I would like at times, but these wilderness wanderings are numerous. A tent is home during such sojourns.

My infatuation with tents and other similar canvas structures goes back to childhood. I fashioned overhead contrivances from practically anything I could find lying around. And I slept in some of these. I actually got my first real tent when I was 12. It was a pyramid rig with a big flap door that could be stretched into a canopy. This unit served me well and was regularly packed with squirming and excited young boys camping in the pasture behind our barn. Grand evenings these were, with us curled under quilts dragged from the house, the sweet aroma of grass drifting up to comfort us. That grass served as our mattress. I have not been without at least one tent since.

When I look into this captivating lure I have for tents and attempt to analyze it to some degree of satisfaction, this in an effort to confirm that I possess a measure of sanity, I must admit to a much-maligned need for escape. There are scoffers at such thinking and practice, you know. I simply listen quietly to them and then go spend a night in my tent.

And do I come away from these mental ramblings and searches for purpose convinced that I am indeed sane? Certainly! I am more persuaded each time I do so. And that generates even more desire to set up a tent.

There are also sensory stimuli common to tent camping that are far more concrete than some obscure need. More tangible, if you will. There is beauty, this coming in large part through symmetry. When I set up camp, or more appropriately when several of us similarly afflicted individuals set up camp, we strive for symmetry, organization. No hodge-podge of scattered items; everything has a place. And all looks pretty much the same: white canvas tents and cook canopies. Each in its designated spot, evenly spaced from another of its kind. All supported by peeled pine poles, not aluminum or fiberglass.

There are blacksmith-made fire tools on which hang buckets and pots, these tools and the blacksmithing courtesy of my friend Neal Brown. There are also ornate masts, made by that same blacksmith, that hold candle and oil lanterns. And while the odd folding chair or table from a big-box store can be seen now and again, the gradual switch to hand-made oak furniture and cypress cook boxes is near complete. This is all quiet, natural beauty that refreshes the battered spirit like nothing else can.

And then there are the sounds. No better way can be found to listen to a cricket chirp or an owl hoot or a coyote yap. Some of these, such as the chirping cricket, may be only inches away from the ear that hears it. But it is still removed by a canvas wall and holds no threat of taking up residence in your sleeping bag. These sounds, all common to night, lull me off to a pleasant and relaxing state that is too often hard to acquire otherwise.

Come daylight the sounds change. But they are abundant just the same: a squirrel barking or shaking a limb, loosing dew drops that splat gently onto the canvas dwelling; a turkey gobbling in the distance; a deer blowing and stamping in disgust at the hulking white edifice and the noxious smell of humanity; wild geese on a morning sun en-route to some faraway environ; the brisk, sharp chirp of a cardinal in search of breakfast. A tent is perfect for absorbing and enjoying such sounds.

Perhaps these are some of the reasons I remain enamored of tents. They are good for the spirit. Day, night – each is equally enchanting. And I am once again reminded that I always sleep best in a tent.

Thoughts on Hunting: A Struggle for Words

Forty years are behind me in the writing business. During that time I have come to realize a truth I heard early on: The greatest fear of a writer is to have an assignment deadline and no words to fill those glaring, threatening blank pages – or computer screens in these more modern times. I recently found myself in that condition. Please indulge me as I explain.

Throughout the entire week in which I was scheduled to contemplate, develop, write, revise, edit and agonize over this very column, I was in a local hospital. I was not the patient. That title belonged to my mother. Still, I was there, as tethered as she to the IVs and obnoxious, beeping monitors and medical staff interruptions. Held captive by a sinister beast that is destroying her cognition, she vacillated between bouts of tears and tremors of fear and required constant supervision. That fell to my sister and me.

But in those rare quiet minutes, I thought. Certainly I thought about my mom and I thought about the situation and how it would eventually play out. But I found pause from time to time to leave that oppressive room, if only in my mind, and think about hunting. For you see, I am a hunter. Have been for more than 50 years. I make that declaration with no apologies and with no agenda to coerce others into the pursuit. It is simply who and what I am: a hunter. And my life has been enriched by it.

I recall those days as a child when my dad took me hunting. Squirrels for the most part. He toted a 20-gauge pump. I trailed behind in childlike fashion. On many occasions he put me on his back as he navigated a briar patch or muddy slough or when going into or coming from the woods before sunrise and after sunset. It was at that time his responsibility to get me through the rough places. But that changed with years. Before I wanted it to happen, it became my responsibility to negotiate the difficult routes, to get through those briars that scratched and stung and through those muddy sloughs that sucked my boots down and held me in the unpleasantness and through those night-time trails that, in my mind at least, hosted the various ghosts of darkness. Not unlike real life, I would say.

And I recall outings during which, both in practice and verbal instruction, I came to embrace and understand the sobriety of life and death. Life was respected, never taken without just cause; death was a reality, always treated with pronounced seriousness. If the animal was not needed, it was not collected. And if it were collected, that was done under the strict confines of legality.

Once, while leaving the squirrel woods, we encountered a covey of quail, these single-filing across a diminutive farm road separating two grass fields. Quail made up a portion of our diet in those days and I wanted to take some for the table. "The season's not open yet. It's three more days till it does," my dad whispered. Three days seemed immaterial to a young hunter under the circumstances. "I won't shoot, but the choice is yours if you want to." A test? Perhaps. He had always stressed the need to obey game laws. That familiar, metallic click, snap of the single barrel's action pushed an unfired .410 shell into my hand.

And one particular fishing trip came to mind. My dad paddled a worn cypress boat along a lake edge and eased into a tiny nook we knew to hold bream. An elderly gentleman was already there, probably no older than I am now but elderly to me then. He was catching fat bluegills with abandon. Dad simply backed away. "Let's get on in there," I offered, my youthful enthusiasm running amuck. "You wouldn't want anybody to do that to you," Dad said. Lesson learned.

Today, I am still a hunter – as I was brought up to be. I thrill to an autumn morning with a stickbow in hand and cedar shafts in my quiver. I even take a deer now and again, this gift meticulously processed and used as winter grows in anger and venison is a prized offering for dinner. But I also relish the experience of simply being in the woods, of hunting. I regularly pull the string taunt, come to anchor and in my mind see that arrow fly to its intended mark, only to ease the string back into brace and smile as the deer continues to nibble. The resultant smile and thanks giving are no less sincere than when an arrow is actually released.

So, I thought in that hospital room as the machines chirped a monotonous, mesmerizing rhythm. I wondered: If it were me there in the bed, engulfed in fears and tears, could I remember those hunting and fishing trips? And if so, would they bring me the same comfort they do now while I yet possess solid recall? I would hope so, for one needs wisdom and the memory of lessons learned and practiced to face such matters. As I gave the entire matter more consideration there on a day that lost its individuality among eight more identical to it, I realized that I had learned all I really needed to know for a full and successful life while fishing and hunting.

A nurse came in and disturbed my reverie.

Pestilence and Pleasure

The country of this place is not big country like that of the Transvaal. The skies are not those big skies of Montana. The vistas here lack that sheer wonderment of those found in the Bitterroot. Remote? Nothing like the Brooks Range. But the inexplicable and almost haunting allure of this place draws me. I never expect to experience again those other places; the prospects of doing so decrease with each passing year. This place, however, outside possible catastrophe or my demise, this place that is unlike most and does not rise to meritorious exoticism as some do, will surely clasp me in its clutches again and again – for as long as I can tug a bow string.

To the west is a sometimes angry river, a river that carries in its turbid flow both life and death, a river that serves up civility and severity in equal measure. It did so this past spring. Its severe mood destroyed; its civil mood enriched. A study in Naturalism – this river. Jack London could well have written about it. William Faulkner did.

To the east are rolling hills. Not mountains; just hills. There are no mountains here. But go far enough northeast in the same state and there waiting are the embryos of mountains, tiny toes of a grander spectacle bearing names such as Smokey and Blue Ridge. Go far enough south and the country has a change of face. It drops into salty waters belonging to the Gulf of Mexico. If the world were flat as once supposed, that southern journey would put the traveler precariously close to the edge.

But this place is none of these. It is sovereign, a separate entity. This Delta. I come here every autumn to hunt deer and flirt with the ghosts of winter. The latter of those two activities is a gentle affair and wholly juvenile. For here, in the South, winter is never and nowhere else in the region as disagreeable as in the Delta. Capricious winds roil across muddy croplands whose black dirt clots with and clings to every step. Those winds fortify their ferocity from open field to open field and seem to fairly rattle scowling skies that more often than not add insult by dribbling rain onto already drowning soil. But my October intrigue is the honeymoon, simply a joyful precursor to winter's mundane reality. And this past October, like many before it, I was there – in this mysterious land where the genteel abundantly melds with the grime.

Neal was there. A decade my junior, he is a treasured companion and as sure to allow an arrow to go where it should on game as any hunter I have ever known. When I turned off the gravel onto a farm road of powder-fine dust shoe-sole deep, he was filling jugs with water at an implement shed. He nodded and said quietly, "The Good Lord just showed out with this day."

We talk like that in the South. Superlatives such as extraordinary or incredible would suffice, but they lose the contest when put up against showed out. I understood his description and concurred. If this ephemeral visual were an accurate indicator, that possible pestilence of the Delta might give way to pure pleasure on this hunt. Then again, the brisk refreshing of this day could simply be distorting past history.

"I'm gonna work on some hides for Charlie," Neal told me as I assisted with lifting the jugs. Charlie allows us access to his property for an annual week-long bowhunt and he had thawed two frozen deer hides from the past season. One would become rawhide, the other a buckskin quiver. We went on around the curve to camp.

No matter how many times I visit this miniscule speck, part of some 5 million altered acres in my home state, I never fail to consider how it all looked before levees and channeling and dredging and chainsaws and bulldozers, before farming overtook the hardwoods. How it smelled and felt and virtually reverberated when decorated with ancient oaks and colossal cypress, these cathedrals of the bottomlands. How it was when the black bear was as ubiquitous as swamp water and coaxed a president and a former slave to align in joint pursuit. The Teddy Bear was born here.

Camp was at its usual location, a quiet grassy spot with cedars and cottonwoods hard against a soybean field. It is now very much home for Neal and me. A pair of white canvas tents greeted us. We would, as the day progressed, locate trails, set up stands, cook a simple supper and shoot our bows.

That latter activity, that very much intoxicating pursuit of sending an arrow from a bow is, I have concluded, closely connected to karate, a discipline I have practiced for years. It is part mental; it is part physical. The muscle memory must be learned and allowed to become part of the whole. But once mastered and nurtured, it is simply there, ready for use when needed. There is little deliberation in setting it free. It is simply unleashed to do its intended chore – the stack and the stance and the chamber mystically similar to the draw and the anchor and the release. Mind and body synchronized minus conscious thought. Mesmerizing.

And trails everywhere! They were narrow guts of barren dirt cut into the leafy forest floor across ridge tops. They were winding strings of hoof prints circumventing a downed tree, victim of some long-past storm. They were visible sign posts of regular travel crossing woods roads and entering edges where mature beans still rested and rattled on browned and withered stalks. Deer were present. The verity of that last statement can at times be tenuous, however, as anyone who possesses a modicum of experience hunting whitetails knows, particularly whitetails in the tangles of the Southeast. There can be every indication of sure action to come, the end result of which giving no credence to elevated expectations. Whitetails are whitetails, the most enthralling and miserably frustrating animal in existence. They play by rules not fully understood by even the most astute observer and pursuer of whitetail truths.

Neal opted for a familiar stand site. Off a ridge in a diminutive bottom with a sand ditch and honey locust tree nearby, this the perfect interlude between Osage and oak and sweet gum bedding thickets to the east. He had taken a beautiful eight point five seasons back and a doe in each of the past two years from this very tree.

I elected, like Neal, a place I knew well. A ridge top above the soybeans with one of those dirt-gut trails slicing the roots of my climbing oak. A big doe was right there just last year when my cedar shaft was launched and flew without fault. The soybeans, a veritable banquet for the deer, lay just down slope.

"Nothing," Neal grunted as we met outside camp after dark. I replied with the same. "Maybe tomorrow," was our unison response.

Tomorrow. Still nothing. We moved stands the next day. That was three of four. And need I even report the confused disbelief served up that day, a sibling of the two before it? Well, if I must. Nothing. Bigfoot would have been no less difficult to locate. And then day four, the last, ended in a clear, glorious sunset that cast its mysterious shadows and gave birth to another Delta night.

What, then, defines the hunt? Is such defining to be reduced to a matter of numbers? If so, that definition is of little consequence, totally inadequate. No, the hunt is far more than numbers, regardless of how these numbers are applied. The hunt, I have now believed for almost three decades, is best defined by the experience. It is this element that is of greatest importance, the factor that more accurately defines us as hunters as well as defining the hunt more completely and deeply than can any collection of numbers. And the experience was fully impressive. This hunt had been of unquestioned benefit.

Independence Day

The setting was a mountain side in Eastern Cape Province, South Africa. I had, hardly an hour before, taken a spectacular kudu bull. This animal was at the top of my want list when I planned the safari, but collecting one hadn't looked too promising up until this point. We had hunted kudu diligently, my professional hunter Deon and I. We had seen a few small bulls and a scattering of cows, but nothing of any great interest. But today, just before light failed, I saw that double helix, those incredible spiraling horns in the distance. When I called Deon's attention to what I believed an apparition, he gasped. "Magnificent bull!" he shouted with an enthusiasm that belied his otherwise mild demeanor.

As best we could, we scrambled through the thorn brush and tangles and over the rock-strewn hillside in an attempt to close the distance. Somehow we accomplished that goal, and as Deon seated the typical African shooting tripod – three bamboo poles lashed together – on the ground and rolled out of the way, the crosshairs settled and the rifle popped. I had my kudu.

After admiring this grandest of all African antelope and paying quiet respect to a fallen monarch, Deon said we should get the truck. This vehicle was two miles away across a rocky stream. Sam and Stan, trackers from a local Swazi tribe, were back that way and would join us in loading the kudu. It seemed only fitting that I stay with the bull, so I broached this possibility. Hesitantly, Deon agreed and walked away. His speedy return was hampered, however. The truck high centered on a rock in the stream, and more than an hour of judicious jacking was required to extricate the rig from its perch.

A bright sun lost purchase in the sky and sank to a mysterious but glorious orange ball on the horizon. The heavens came alive with night, typical of Africa. The Milky Way was at my fingertips; the Southern Cross dangled amid a firmament rich with wonder. This was winter in the Southern Hemisphere, and cold air rushed from the peaks. I stroked that coarse coat of the kudu and shed tears of gratitude for the bull and the day and the experience. Surreal.

Suddenly an epiphany: This was July 4th. Independence Day. The first since that September 11th incident that shocked the United States. Though night had fallen in eastern Africa, noon had not yet come back home. Ribs and chicken would be on the grill in preparation for a holiday feast. Someone somewhere had a watermelon in a tub of ice water. Fireworks would crackle.

Then night sounds shook off my reverie. Startling and menacing. Strange and sinister. Unnerving if for no other reason than they were unidentifiable to one not familiar with them. Night had come; the hunt had begun. Death for some would give life to others. I shuddered, in part from the cold and in part from an element of fear.

But with the meaning of this day in mind, my thoughts turned to its deep significance. I imagined Washington's troops during the Revolution. I concluded they likely shuddered at the sound of musket fire and the thud of cannon. I imagined my dad and my uncle and thousands of others like them in France and Italy, on Omaha Beach and Iwo Jima. They likely shuddered at the clatter of machine gun and the burst of mortar shell and the thunder of bomb.

Closer in time to that African evening, I remembered those

friends who trudged the tunnels and humid tangles of Vietnam, two of whom I had rabbit hunted with in the winter before a sniper's bullet the following spring ended any potential held in those young lives. All these must have shuddered. Some lived to re-call it; some did not.

In no small way, these, and many even now, provided me the freedom and privilege of being exactly where I wanted to be, when I wanted to be there – in Africa. I considered the debt I owed and again shed tears.

Sitting there on that mountain side, I searched for words to whisper across the lonely darkness to God, to Africa, to the animals, and to those individuals who gave so much. Only two seemed ap-propriate; I chanted them repeatedly: "Thank you." That was a poignant and unique Independence Day.

Making Ready

Ahead and down slope a few yards is a stream. Too small to be considered a creek, it is what the old folks from my childhood called a branch. This one is Cannon Branch, a miniscule trickle that I can hop across at practically any point. But a stream with some sandy edges along its route. I see tracks there. I think I can identify them from my station but opt to move in for a better look. I step closer and bend low to the sand.

A grey squirrel. Just what I thought. He probably stopped here for a drink and then scurried up that old hickory there. The hickory's leaves are red and yellow and glowing in an early October sun. The nuts are blackened, their leathery coats shriveled with the close of summer. Cuttings at the hickory's base show that bushytails have been having a jolly good time there.

And then a sound – a raucous, almost unnerving noise that causes me to startle briefly before full recognition sinks in. At that I smile. The call of a pileated woodpecker is boisterous, but at the same time it is somehow soothing. My dad called them Indian Hens. Everyone from the area where I grew up called them Indian Hens. Their dancing, up-and-down flight, and haunting cry have been a part of my being for as long as I can remember. The birds are a symbol of wildness in these parts.

There was a time when I would ask nothing more than locating squirrel sign and hearing an Indian Hen. These signaled the genesis of autumn, the beginning of hunting season; that is what I lived for. I still do, and those prognosticators are yet viable. But it is more than squirrel cuttings and bird call I seek. Bow season is open and I want to find that perfect stand location. I step across Cannon Branch.

Down just a few more yards I find that spot. A trail leads from a thicket and into a cluster of oaks, their leaves that were deep green in July now faded and brittle and spangled with color. Their sweet gum cousins are even more brilliant. Yellow, red, orange – these afford a visual feast. One sweet gum leaf looses from its perch and drifts downward, bumping others of its kind. Coupled with the chirp of katydids and grasshoppers, it is a symphony as fine as any from Beethoven.

A corn field is there in the distance a ways. Its knurled stalks and twisted leaves rattle in a tender breeze from the north. A crow calls. I climb a strong oak that provides cover.

And then that familiar crunch. A wide-eyed doe picks up an early acorn. I push the longbow to arm's length and apply pressure to the string. I shiver. Must be the chill of late afternoon, I think. After all, fall is in the air.

Myth, Legend, Fact, Fiction

The outdoor world is filled with stories that have been passed down through generations. The validity of some tales may come into question when carefully researched, but still they remain, holding a great deal of perceived truth for those who hear and/or pass them along.

As a child I heard many a tall tale from the older residents of our community. They repeated these with strong conviction. Some of the most startling and enduring stories focused on snakes. It seemed at times that the yarn spinners were obsessed with snakes. Although a young outdoorsman and farm boy, I was never privileged to encounter any of these creatures, but I was assured by those around me that the beings did indeed exist and that I would be wise to avoid them. My favorite was and still is the stinging snake.

According to what I heard, the stinging snake was a hideous thing that preferred to remain buried in the mud of sloughs and stream sides. The hapless woods guest who was unfortunate enough to step on one of these was sure to be stung repeatedly about the feet and ankles, this resulting in the quick demise of that one so afflicted. One elderly gentleman told of seeing a man wade off into the Pearl River for an afternoon swim near where we lived. He was immediately attacked by hordes of stinging snakes.

He went under and was never seen again.

Another man claimed to have encountered a stinging snake in some weeds. Angered by this man's disturbance, the snake chased the man around a bit but was unable to connect. The snake, apparently in full frustration, jabbed that wicked stinger into a pine tree, which subsequently withered and died.

There was another snake of great import in stories circulating about our community – the coach whip. Some pronounced it coarch whip. This one was rumored to chase its victim down, wrap around a leg or arm or neck, and then proceed to give the individual a thorough lashing with the long tail.

And it could have been this one that also possessed another curious trait. Then again, this next might have been another vicious serpent; I don't recall. But whether it was the coach whip or something else often called the hoop snake, the purveyors of propaganda said that it would grasp its tail in its mouth to form a hoop so that it could roll like a wheel in an effort to more quickly close the distance on its intended target, the latter being young lads who had wandered into areas they were told to avoid. Scary stuff, this.

Owls have long played an integral role in folklore. One species that was of particular interest in my area was the diminutive screech owl. A curious little critter, the screech owl has a haunting, unnerving cry. It is not a hoot like other owls; the call is distressing, mournful. No wonder this bird is considered a bad omen.

Legend has it – or did in my youth among the neighbors – that a screech owl calling outside a dwelling at night meant disaster would fall on that household within a few days. Individuals who heard that eerie call would go outside with a pan and spoon or similar noise maker to frighten the owl away. Some even fired a shotgun into the air to cause the owl to move on. It was all very sobering.

And we can't forget pranks related to the outdoors. Young boys out on a first camping trip were sure to be greeted at some point during the night by the dumb bull. This would usually send them packing, never to return until the tricksters came clean and explained the situation. The dumb bull was nothing more than a coffee can or syrup bucket or some such with a nail hole punched in the bottom. Through this hole was run a length of heavy string coated with pine resin. Stripping this string through the fingers produced a raucous roar unlike anything the young ones had heard. It generally put the boys to flight and left the prank players in fits of boisterous laughter.

Stinging snakes, coach whips, screech owls, dumb bulls and a host of other entities – these were common in my youth. Were they real? They were real enough to keep a collection of country boys in line!

Last Sunrise From the Blind

That sunrise was spectacular. At first there was only a hint of orange, but it morphed gently into a golden glow, quickly pursuing the darkness. Fingers of light pushed through fog and mist and sent bright tentacles bouncing across muddy fields and puddles, challenging the cold with a promise of tolerable warmth. Winter wind burnished plant stubble and exposed fingers; ripples from its attack danced across flooded soybeans.

And as light began to gain purchase in an otherwise grey sky, the sound came. It was a low honking that was at first faint and nondescript. But as its intensity grew, now accompanied by wings opting for altitude and cutting the cold, it became a haunting rumble that put one in mind of distant thunder. Geese, thousands upon thousands, were beginning their day. They fairly blackened the sky to the north and west. They soared high over the blinds in boisterous flocks, their huge "Vs" a phenomenon of nature that causes one to stare in amazement at their grace, their intent, their resolve. A humbling experience it is to watch such a spectacle while bound so completely to Earth as we are.

Then other birds took flight. Doves, in singles and pairs and flocks of a dozen or more, darted here and there with blinding speed. In contrast, a heron drifted by right to left barely above the water in a slow-motion effort that allowed its head to remain vertically stationary while its body rose and fell in rhythm with the powerful, steady beats of long wings. A flock of starlings skittered about on the horizon. A hawk screamed in the distance.

And there were ducks. Mallards flew overhead, voicing that throaty, croaking quack common to the species. Shovelers circled the decoy spread, their wide bills giving credence to the name. Teal, tiny and football shaped, zipped through the tangle of other waterfowl with great agility. Two pintails made a pair of wide passes but were not enticed to move closer. The air was alive.

From time to time shotguns rumbled. An occasional duck plummeted from the company of his kin and splashed onto the water, this one immediately retrieved and placed beside the blinds gently and with reverence – as it should be. When one dropped, dozens, perhaps hundreds, flared upward and into the heavens.

At some point I came to realize that this was the last sunrise from the blind. Season was ending; there would be no more mornings this year for participation in such a grand pursuit. And then I pondered the possibility of this being, in the most final sense, the last sunrise from the blind. If it were and if I were aware of that fact, what would I wish for? What would I change?

I would, as I suppose most of us would, wish for more opportunities to see the sunrise. I would wish for another chance to feel the wind bite at my face, to hear the whistle of wings through the morning mist, to see bird life in all its varied forms begin a new day. I would wish for more time with friends, companions who share the same drive as I, who appreciate that same sense of awe inspired by the natural world. I would wish for more campfires.

I would wish to feel the cold steel and warm wood of a battered shotgun that has felt the same discomfort, exhilaration and joy mingled with sadness as I – if indeed it can feel as I suspect a favorite shotgun can. To hold close by my side this entity that now seems to understand my idiosyncrasies even better than I understand its mechanical workings. To feel its bump of recoil against my shoulder. To sight down that ribbed barrel and experience the present as I recall the past and dream of the future. Yes, I would wish for more days.

And regarding that last sunrise of the season I was enjoying from the blind as these thoughts drifted through my mind: What would I change? Absolutely nothing. Change offers little enhancement to perfection.

Taking Leave; Stepping Back

What is it about nostalgia that is so terribly appealing? The question is easily asked, and I hear it often. But the responses suitable for answering such a perplexing probe are remarkably difficult to formulate. There simply are too many variables.

Age is one cause for this somewhat misplaced longing. Years forward tend to dim the truth of years past, and we may wish things could be as they were in the good old days. There is merit in such thinking. Yesterday was a time of simplicity. Today, however, is filled with complexity. That could hold true regardless of the era, for the 19th Century was likely more complex than the 18th, particularly for those whose lives spanned some of both. And the 20th Century was increasingly more complex than the 19th, and so on. You, I am sure, grasp the process here outlined. So, it is not fully unnatural to desire a simple, less hectic world. But we live in the world of today and perhaps tomorrow, not in yesterday. Still, we ache and wonder for much of what has slipped past, many times unnoticed until it no longer exists.

Age aside, there is still a powerful lure associated with the past. It is evidenced in those far younger than I who become curious about people of the past and the lives they lived. Just this past Saturday evening, as this is written, I was privileged to present my

18th Century program for a large group at Moselle Baptist Church in Jones County. Among the 500 or so there, a great many were young people – children, teens, young adults. All listened intently. They fondled long-hunter shirts and a wool capote and a canvas greatcoat and forged knives and copper corn boilers and buckskin moccasins and a flintlock rifle. They were enthralled by a flint-and-steel fire kit. They touched a heavy wool blanket rolled onto a tump line, a system and product exactly like that used by such personalities as Daniel Boone in 1770. They admired my battered and stained leggings over canvas knee breeches, both now showing extensive wear from a decade of heavy use.

And last week I set up and tended a booth for Primitive Archer magazine at the Pre-Spring Arrow Fling at Tannehill State Historical Park near Birmingham. Again, there were hundreds in attendance, many of them youngsters and most shooting the target ranges. Others just curious. This is a traditional-only gathering, and some truly impressive glass-and-wood recurves were in use, these true works of art. But there was also an increasing number of all-wood bows in various styles, another step back in time. My own Osage and bamboo longbow backed with copperheads, coupled with a Plains-Style leather quiver decorated with feathers and beads and holding cedar arrows, gave pause for each passerby to stop and stare. Wonderment filled their eyes, and many had to ask how it performed. Quite wonderfully, I must say. Remember, Native Americans fed entire villages with the sweet meat of bison taken with such gear.

Events such as these two mentioned convince me more completely each time I attend them that there is something inherent in many that prompts them to explore the past. Why and what? I still don't know for sure. But for me it is the reward of being more closely in touch with self and the environment. It is the requirement that I rely more on myself and my companions than on technology and gadgetry. It is the realization that I can be content with very little, can live a full life minus the external stimuli of obnoxious noise and the latest contrivances touted by advertising as essential. It is reaching the experienced conclusion that had I been one from the past, I could have, as they did, survived the normal and regular hardships of a difficult but simple life. Plus, it is all fun – this playing the Old Days game.

And these are all ample justification to take leave of today and step back to yesterday from time to time.

Antelope Magic

Magic permeates a chilly breeze that drifts over sage brush. Couple that with a big Sharps rifle, and the visitor thus located and equipped becomes part of a surreal world, one foreign to modernity. The world this one enters is that of fringed leather jackets and shaggy beasts, their pronounced humps and ponderous heads rising and falling in the distance like dark waves on a truculent sea. A world of rugged individualism. A world serenaded by the lonesome call of coyotes. A world punctuated by the black periods and hyphens emitting from smokestacks of early steam engines. A world that has clearly passed from existence, fully available only in the imagination. But such surroundings prompt imagination!

That concept of a new world meeting an old was in my mind as the small jet approached Casper, Wyoming, one early October evening. There would be no shaggy beasts on the agenda. There would be no smoke from coal-fired steam engines. But there would be the cry of coyotes. There would be a Sharps rifle, as well as a rolling block. And there would be antelope, easily my personal favorite among North America's myriad of big game animals.

Cabela's Communications Specialist David Draper met four of us at the airport: Alan Clemmons, Dave Henderson, Mark Olis, and me, all of whom are involved in the business of spinning outdoor yarns for various publications. Ann Smith and Stephanie

Mallory were already in camp, this located not far from the town of Glen Rock. The hunt had been arranged with Angie and Scott Denny of Table Mountain Outfitters (P.O. Box 2714, Cheyenne, WY, 82003; 307-632-6352; www.TableMountainOutfitters.com). The Dennys' operation covers a broad spectrum of hunting opportunities and provides reliable service and accommodations.

All hunters were using Cabela's clothing and footwear: Open Country and Outfitter camo, orange vests, and the 8-inch Silent Stalker Sneakers in Mossy Oak Break Up. And while lacking the nostalgic appeal of leather coats and ragged cowboy boots, the attire was purely grand for the chore at hand. I particularly appreciated the sneakers as the trip wore on, and I am now a true fan of Cabela's Microtex.

Dave Henderson and I opted for the rolling block and 1874 Sharps, respectively, both in .45-70 and both of the Cabela's persuasion. All others carried some new-fangled scoped centerfires, but I reminded them regularly that when compared to black powder, smokeless was simply a passing fad!

Some might wonder at the choice of open-sighted rifles in such a caliber as .45-70 for antelope. This game is generally a long-range affair, and it can be argued that a great many more modern units will do the job better. But one who would consider such a thing probably would not understand any spoken explanation, for the reason goes much deeper than words. There is history. There is a longing for something other than the present. There is wonder, curiosity. There is grandeur. There is class! No, words can't fully express these things. They must be experienced, absorbed deeply into the very being of the user. These rifles simply seemed like the thing to do.

There can be no questioning the effectiveness of rigs such as those Dave and I toted. Any trepidation can find respite in the tales of buffalo hunters. Equipped with tang sights and with barrels resting between shooting sticks or over sage brush, these rifles took down thousands of bison. If range were established in a reasonable fashion, antelope should be no particular obstacle.

That first morning was the type that is never forgotten once it is encountered: a brisk wind chilling the air to the point of producing shivers; a shy sun peeking around buttes and through sage and creeping into coulees and reflecting off the fans of distant windmills. It was a grand day to be alive and to be in the Wyoming countryside. And there were antelope.

The first one we located holding interest for guide Tom Groves and me was enamored of five or six does on a hillside some 400 yards out. A view through the spotting scope proved him worthy of our attention, and we laid plans for a possible approach. Unlike much of the antelope hunting I have enjoyed, this episode proved almost too easy. Within 20 minutes or so we were in a profitable position as I readied a rest from my backpack and admired the buck through the tang sight. "A hundred and 26 yards," Tom said after a quick read of the rangefinder. That was no real proposition, and I lamented the fact that my hunt would end so soon on this glorious morning. With the sight dialed to perfection and the front post residing on that spot behind the shoulder where the color change occurs on pronghorns, I set the back trigger and applied gentle pressure to the front.

At that moment there was the magic. A blue/grey cloud of putrid smoke from the Goex load drifted away on a Wyoming wind. Smug, I was – until I realized that something was dreadfully wrong. The antelope was not down, was not even faltering. He was speeding away with grace and agility, always keeping his does corralled and close. I had missed! Shot high.

For those who have experienced such blatant defeat at their own hands, there is little need here to attempt an explanation of my sentiment. I was discouraged, confused, frustrated. Here was I – the gun crank, the one who had touted the suitability of a Sharps, the one who had highlighted his shooting prowess with said rifle –

standing there in abject poverty of pride and confidence, no chance remaining to make a good first impression on a gracious guide. The episode would not be easily or quickly rectified.

Not long afterward, two worlds met in obvious discord. As soon as we arrived at the truck, a cell phone jangled us from the past to the present, temporarily interrupting my reverent mental journey into the late 19th Century and momentarily extracting me from my state of despondency. Word was that Dave Henderson and his big rolling block had met with success on another ranch. He had crawled toward a ridge containing a buck, and the buck had obliged. The range was 96 yards, Dave's aim more precise than mine. I was glad for his success, glad that he had shown what the old rifles could do – in the same manner they had done generations earlier.

On around a ranch road and down near a small drainage, Tom spotted antelope. This was not especially noteworthy, for antelope were just about everywhere we looked; it had been that way since daylight. What was significant about this particular find was that there were three highly impressive bucks present in the vicinity, one outstanding. And the terrain looked friendly. This thing just might work out.

Approximately a half-hour later Tom and I were atop a butte, observing bucks as they sorted does. There was little chance of moving closer, but there was the distinct possibility that in their rambling and jousting, antelope might drift within range. Save a strong wind that was at times disagreeable, this spot was about as pleasant as any on Earth; consequently, we opted to hold and permit the drama to play out. No boredom. Action was constant and the scenery more than splendid.

I hesitate to hazard a guess regarding how long we lay there in the Wyoming sunshine; a timepiece seemed an affront to the moment. But probably no more than 45 minutes passed before antelope began to trickle into a depression above which Tom and I were stationed. One of the three bucks we had been watching was there. Things happened quickly from that point on, and before much discussion or planning had been implemented, the buck was clear of his associates and broadside.

"A hundred and 89 yards," Tom told me, this his second time to do the ranging and apprising me of the situation. The Sharps was resting in the sticks and the front sight dancing against the buck. But rather than settle into a practiced regimen that I knew well and completing the process, I allowed my mind to drift back to that missed shot earlier and I hesitated. The buck moved. Not far and not quickly but gradually, until Tom's accurate reporting dissuaded me: "212; 241; 263!" The buck was walking out of my life – perhaps forever.

Lunch, maybe a bit late, was refreshing and welcomed. But it was also somber, that is the mood was. Tom glassed over near the edge of the hill; I reflected with glum recall on the morning. But this all was to be short lived. We would soon move on and make another attempt on a buck. And another and another if needed. I had missed; most all of us have. That episode could not be the definitive moment of this hunt.

Over there, just down the hill from a vantage point we occupied, was something. Low to the ground. Stationary in a landscape of wind-buffeted grass. Not an antelope. A mule deer buck. He was bedded and peaceful. And he afforded another occasion to admire and give thanks and pause in reverence.

Now, on down the ridge. Way out. Over there where those two fences corner. There, darting back and forth like diminutive apparitions were antelope. The unaided eye made them out for nothing more than pronghorns, but the spotting scope gave a more complete and detailed account. "That's the buck you missed," Tom told me. Close observation verified this, and it was clear that he was with the does that had accompanied him earlier. The group had moved from a long ridge and down into a small creek bottom not too terribly far from my foiled attempt several hours prior. And they were now picking their way back up, toward that spot of initial contact. We were off!

The pickup was employed to move us with more haste than walking would have afforded, and we abandoned it somewhere on the off-side of the ridge after reaching a position that we reckoned would put us in a favorable location to intercept the pronghorns should they continue their trek. Binoculars verified that our decision was a wise one.

The Wyoming sun was already casting haunting shadows as we bent-over walked and crawled in an effort to gain some advantage. The late afternoon air was regaining its bite of early morning. With thoughts of my mishap still plaguing my resolve, I checked the tang sight and exercised a long list of mental gymnastics that should put the big bullet where it must go. And then it was time. The buck was there, just short of breaking into a narrow opening in the sage that would make him viable. Again, Tom was at his job of assistance by calling the distance; "159 yards," he whispered.

All experienced hunters know the status of this condition. It is the territory of slow motion, the province of a dream-like state, the locale where all else vanishes save the game and the rifle and the sight picture and the trigger pull. The resultant blast, smoke, and recoil take the shooter quite by surprise, as these should. And all experienced hunters know when the entire thing has worked as planned. There is the "whump" of the bullet strike, the reaction of the animal. These were present, but barely breaking the spell cast only seconds before.

And there was the antelope buck, lying still at the base of a big clump of sage. Even in that posture he was majestic. Black horns and tawny-on-white coat. A symbol of wildness, a fixture of this marvelous landscape, a gift from the Creator who made all. And the magic was there – on the breeze that drifts over sage brush. I stopped and gave thanks.

Passing on the Infatuation, Instruction, and Pleasure

The hunter in me encourages a minor episode of melancholy at this time of year. Those long-anticipated seasons that occupied my mind and spare time in September are soon to be a memory for another year. Yes, there is a West Texas hunt and magazine assignment that will be completed before you read this. And there are a few more treks planned for the squirrel woods during February, my favorite hunting activity. Turkey season will roll around in March. Then there is even another African adventure and magazine project that will occur in mid-summer as I push through thorn bush, wooden longbow in hand, and search for that magnificent Grey Ghost of the rocky tangles, the kudu. All grand dealings. But those five months of being free to ramble in Mississippi with a prodigious list of open seasons available are ending soon.

As I look back on the outdoor experiences that will become memories within a few days, I am reminded of the good derived from them all. I put a deer in the freezer but watched in wide-eyed amazement and deep gratitude as countless more of these marvelous creatures simply went about doing what deer do. There was no cause to draw the bow or cock the hammer on my rifle. Watching was the greater reward. But perhaps the greatest reward of the

2012-2013 seasons was spending time with my great nephew Bo – the closest thing I have to a son or grandson. He is becoming quite the hunter.

And he took a deer one cold afternoon in late December. Other than being with him, I was not involved. He spotted the deer first and I sat in silent observation. I saw him squirm into position and coax a too-big rifle to his shoulder. I studied him closely as he made sure he had the proper hold and sight picture. I marveled at his calmness and patience in the midst of excitement. After the shot I smiled in approval as he quietly extracted the spent case and poked the remaining thumb-sized rounds back into the magazine and slid the bolt closed over them to assure the chamber was empty before he moved the muzzle. I saw that glint of sobering sadness peek through the enchantment. I feel that same heart tug when I do as he did.

To be truthful – and selfish to a degree – I hope some of what he demonstrated was the result of my training over the past two or three years in similar settings. Or perhaps these practices came from long conversations he and I have had regarding safety and respect and what it really means to hunt and ultimately take an animal. Or maybe it is just his compassionate nature. There is a possibility that I had nothing to do with it all. But whatever the impetus, he seems to have learned well.

But that deer was not the only thing of great import on this outing. We talked in a whispered manner about his future. I learned more of his dreams and gave encouragement to strive for them. He even asked my opinion on the type and caliber rifle he should get. I outlined a variety that might be considered and instructed him to make his own decision based on practicality rather than misguided publicity. We talked of his friendships and how these can and do influence his own life. We talked of God's creation and its marvels. I was pleased with his insight.

He asked about my adventures in various venues. I told

him, as I have before, of a lonesome and haunting late afternoon and early evening alone on a South African koppie as I sat and shivered with cold and excitement and a pronounced degree of trepidation as unfamiliar night sounds filled the air and the Milky Way engulfed me. I told him of my attempt to stay aboard a spooked saddle horse as he ran through tamarak and spruce in an attempt to put distance between himself and a grizzly. The horse had no regard for me! I told him of a Montana blizzard that put four of us inside a big canvas tent for three days in the Missouri Breaks. I told him of growing up with very little and yet experiencing a true form of wealth while beside my dad in the Pearl River swamps hunting squirrels for supper. Those latter remain the grandest memories of them all.

The weather was cold that day Bo and I went hunting. But never did I hear a complaint. Never once did he suggest we go home, nor did he have his pack stuffed with electronic gadgets. He was there to hunt. And he did it with proper style. "I want to do all those things you have done," he said. Perhaps he can.

Bo and I have a campout and squirrel hunt planned in February.

Closing Mississippi's Season with Bo

We have camp secure, Bo and I. Housing is a David Ellis Range Tent, a 10 x 10 suspended by peeled-pine poles. Inside are foam sleeping pads, sleeping bags, a pair of wool blankets and an olive-oil lamp. This latter will flicker its mystical glow well into the night as I attempt to answer with clarity and sincerity Bo's grandiose questions about the hunting world and my many experiences in it, these now encompassing more than 50 years. Goodness, time has done anything but creep.

Outside the tent is a canvas fly, this also 10 x 10. It will serve as a place to sit while a small 18th Century brazier emits its diminutive but warming flame just beyond the fly's eve. Two oak-and-rope holders nestle containers of water, one for hand washing and one for drinking and making coffee. There is also a two-piece oak table that I envisioned one late night when I should have been sleeping. I built it so that it would slide together on either side of the fly's middle pole, thus producing more usable space under that fly. I also built the oak-and-rope holders so that they fold into a compact package for travel. Somewhat favoring a throwback to antiquity, the camp is highly functional. I like things that way, old and functional. No new gadgets to clutter one's mind. I hope Bo will like such systems as much as I.

I have been watching Bo since camp was set. He split with a hatchet some fat pine kindling into usable splinters. These I will employ to start the evening fire. He is now tinkering with his new .22 rifle. Quite the marksman he has become. And safe, too. Not once during my observation have I seen him abandon prescribed protocol. I worry little about him now in that regard. And those same splinters split today will serve well tomorrow. For it is then that I will teach him the fascinating tactic of starting fire with flint and steel and char cloth. He needs to know that. His survival could depend upon such skills. But even if it never does, he needs to know so that he can understand what it means to be self-sufficient and will know how it was done by individuals long ago.

*****

Another day has slipped quietly over the pines. We slept well last night. I heard Bo stir but once, and this hardly noticed. He did so when a collection of coyotes wailed a plaintive song near camp. Though signaling little danger, this sound still causes chills, perhaps because of its wildness as opposed to its threat. Today we will end another season, and my young companion will try his hand at the flint and steel. We will cook breakfast over the fire he generates. All has been well.

Bo is growing up. The nature of that process is change, and I am sure he will. But I hope the whirlwind of young adulthood will be kind to him. I hope he will still want to strike fire with flint and steel and char cloth and sleep in canvas tents and move quietly though the squirrel woods. Those decisions are his and time will reveal the outcome. I hope I have done my best. And I look forward to the others: Grant and Carson and Ford and Ethan. All, like Bo, are great nephews, but I could never have had sons or grandsons who would be more entrenched into my very core than these. Boys, to each of you, all the best this life has to offer.

In Search of Myself

The setting is virtually silent. Save a gentle gurgle where river water pours over a log jam and the cold rustle of January wind through cypress and disrobed willows, there is quiet. But that is good. There is far too little silence in this world.

I am looking for wood ducks. The drone of that tiny outboard that propelled my passage to this spot had caused a steady eruption of woodies. They burst from clear waters at every bend and tangle, their high-pitched squeal filling the air, those gaudy colors flashing in a winter sun. And now I am at Jennings Hole, the exact locale that marks my beginning as an outdoorsman.

And then there is the smell. It is pungent but pleasant. It comes from the mud and decaying debris left behind by high water, and its sting pushes me back to childhood. I recall stories of the Jennings Hole, tales that came from my dad of the days he lived on the bluff above the river and unearthed stumps and plowed mules in cotton patches that then filled the flat, rich earth. I don't recall the first time he took me there; I was a young child. But it was important to him that I know, that the history and the river become a part of my being. This happened, completely.

However, I do recall that warm May morning he took me in a cypress boat to Jennings Hole and handed me a cane pole. There was a goose-quill bobber and diminutive hook and split shot on the line. The cricket had barely hit the water when a belligerent bluegill attacked. This battle was long, but the bream eventually plopped to the boat's bottom. I was enthralled then and am now at the memory.

Reverie is disturbed by the hiss of wings. I blink away tears that I credit to the cold and see a woodie drake and duet of hens. I pull a battered A-5 to my shoulder and the drake splashes to the rippled surface. Even in this posture he is magnificent. Recall enters a second time.

I see my dad sitting close to me, his tan and tattered shell vest over a worn denim jacket. "He's right there," Dad whispered as he pointed out a squirrel in a double-trunk pine on the bluff. The bluff and pine are still here, just as they were then. The .410 popped. The river and its surrounding had again worked their magic.

I sit here and admire the drake that I have just taken and realize that I was not seeking ducks this morning as much as I was seeking self. I found what I had gone after.

At times I think my blood is diluted with that river water, made richer by its flow. And while it may seem morbid, I don't think I would mind if my ashes were scattered along the Pearl when that time comes. Seems only fitting, for a river, that river, runs through me.

Plans and Hopes

The fall/winter hunting seasons are behind us. I am always in that position of dichotomy at this time each year. I am sorry to see those deer and squirrel and rabbit seasons close, but I am glad to have the opportunity to move on to spring and summer endeavors. And I have a long list of those planned – if I can make the time and remain healthy and see to the caregiving of parents and meet the other demands of everyday life without becoming delinquent in such responsibilities. Most readers can relate to those contingencies.

The first in that list of plans is to work diligently on some black-powder cartridge loads for my Sharps rifle. That rig, the Model 1874 chambered to the venerable .45-70, was the rifle during the great bison hunts of the two decades following the Civil War. We know of that infamous time now as one of wasteful tragedy in which herds numbering in the millions were practically exterminated. Sad as that is to us, it was a colorful time in the history of westward movement, and the Sharps rifle and ponderous American buffalo are an integral part of that history.

We can celebrate the recovery of the bison today, and we can again acquire a Sharps rifle in its initial form, made in Big Timber, Montana. So the bison and Sharps can once again be paired up with no threat to the demise of that species of great beast.

And that is why I will work on those black-powder loads for the Sharps – a bison hunt in October, set on the prairies just outside Dodge City, Kansas. Throw in lodging in a tipi, horses for travel, a fringed leather jacket to chase the cold, and you have the makings of a nostalgic Old West experience. And whether the trip is a success or failure in regards to taking a bison is of no great consequence. It is the experience that will be remembered.

I also plan to turkey hunt. Want to take one with an Osage and bamboo stickbow and stone-tipped arrow. Got closer than I ever imagined I would this past spring. Perhaps this one will be the time I accomplish that goal.

And I want to fish some. Bream mostly. I grew up doing that and love it. Haven't done much in the past 20 years, but plans are to change that situation. Maybe circumstances will allow that to happen.

Plans, hopes – all these. Will they become reality? Time will tell. But whether I get to do those things or not is somewhat immaterial. The dreams are there. Hope is alive. Life is in the hands of One far greater than humanity. I plan to rest in that certainty.

Aging and the Complexities of Life

Life is often complex. We all experience that need for a little smoothing of the edges from time to time. That is what archery has done for me practically all my life. It never removed the complexities, but it did definitely smooth those rough edges each time it was employed.

For the better part of this past year, I have found myself gradually growing deeper into primary caregiving for parents, ages 86 and 88. That is ongoing. The future is uncertain, but a logical conclusion is that none of this will end soon. The chores will become even more pronounced as days pass. Many of you identify; you have done the same or are doing the same. And you know the responsibilities are gladly met. To do otherwise would trouble our spirits, disturb dignity. But you also know those responsibilities can be tiring, emotionally draining.

A great portion of that drain is the simple task of watching, seeing those we care about and who have cared for us decline in abilities to live life as they, and we, have known it. My mother was always the one to congratulate my dad and me when we came home with fish or game. Such ingredients were an essential part of our food supply when I was growing up. We had little more than what we grew or took from the waters, woods and fields around home. It was my mother who always reminded us that we were important and essential. It was she who watched with a smile and spoke with a kind voice as we pulled a collection of wild foods from tattered vests or sacks. There are now days when she doesn't know where she is when she wakes. Can't recall the names of her church friends.

And my dad? Always robust and strong. He had more hair at 75 than I did at 50. It was he who brought home a single-barrel shotgun when I was 12 and showed me how to use it. It was he who took me to the squirrel woods and quail fields, always giving me the first shot. Or second if I needed it. It was he who ordered my first bow and cedar arrows from Sears somewhere around 1958. It was, clearly and without question, he who inspired and taught and encouraged me in the ways of wild things. He was a master.

Now he is stooped. Now he stumbles and totters about. Now his hands will hardly allow the turning of pages. Now his shotguns have been in the rack for two decades. Now his fishing poles have decayed and rusted away. Grievous.

And I look at myself. First it was arthritis. Then came a dysfunctional shoulder. After that, a vertebra that had to be fused. Now it is a second shoulder. And the arthritis continues to work its sinister doings. All these ailments have, for a time, interrupted my archery, but each passed and I was able to return to this grandest of all endeavors.

I now realize that I am, as we say in the country, no longer a spring chicken! Could it be that archery is, much against my wishes, exiting my life? I have steadily reduced weights: 62 to 60 to 55 to 50. Could it be 45 is next? Could it be that I will very soon no longer be able to shoot at all? Perhaps. But then how do I smooth those jagged edges that life brings?

Maybe showing a new convert to primitive ways how to build an arrow will suffice. Maybe coaching my great nephew on his draw and release will do it. Maybe. These will certainly keep me in-volved. But none of these will have the same impact as feeling Osage in my hand. None will accomplish the smoothing of rough edges as does absorbing the mystique of a cedar shaft gliding to-ward its target. But maybe none of these alternatives will be neces-sary for a few more years. We deal with life's complexities as they come.

A Tribute to Barlow

Barlow was not my dog, but he was definitely my friend. A mountain cur, Barlow belonged to my constant hunting companion Neal Brown, a retired State Trooper who is as mad about stick bows and 18th Century flintlocks and buckskin leggings as I am. The two of us often say, "If it is not old, we don't like it!"

And Barlow liked it. He was the perfect squirrel dog and camping buddy. When Neal and I were hunting, Barlow was all business, never failing in his integrity. If he treed, a squirrel was there. But when the hunt was over or we stopped for a break, Barlow was there, begging a bit of head patting or a piece of venison sausage we were cooking on a green stick over a woods fire. And he would curl up in a canvas tent for the night, disturbing no one save with an occasional sigh of tremendous delight.

Barlow met no stranger. When I drove up to Neal's – or when anyone else did for that matter – he came out jumping and yapping with glee. He was always glad to see a visitor. And if you sat long enough, he would keep nudging closer until, if you allowed, he had his lanky, muscular frame draped across your lap.

I recall one hunt several years back when Neal and I, flintlocks in hand and dressed in 18th Century attire, were in the Yockanookany Swamp. Squirrels were not cooperating particularly well, but Barlow suddenly treed on a broken oak that left behind an eight-foot-high stump. We looked it over carefully, but to no avail.

"I believe Barlow's lying to us for the first time," Neal noted. But a bit of bumping and searching revealed otherwise. A squirrel scooted from the broken top and Neal took him quite handily with a .32-caliber ball from his flinter. Barlow continued. While Neal was reloading, a second squirrel scampered from that same locale and made it to another tree. It was my turn to produce a cloud of putrid black-powder smoke from a .32. The squirrel dropped. Barlow had maintained his record of reliability.

Neal tells a humorous story about Barlow that I missed seeing. Neal had gone to the swamp in early fall to check for deer sign, and Barlow was naturally perched on the back of Neal's four wheeler. While Neal was scouting, he missed Barlow. But he soon heard him coming through the woods issuing a most unusual bark. Curious, Neal began scanning the woods to see what was taking place. He soon saw Barlow running full tilt and yapping, while a big doe was hot on his tail. Apparently Barlow had encountered the doe and perhaps her fawn and the doe would have nothing of that. Barlow made it to the four wheeler and jumped up onto the rack. The doe skidded to a halt, looked, snorted, and then disappeared in the direction from where she had come. Barlow never had any use for deer – before or after!

I visited Neal day before yesterday, just three days after he had built a pine box for Barlow and laid him in the hillside sod behind the house. We will miss him tremendously. But while I was there, Boss and Sugar Bear, two pups Barlow sired, were busying themselves about the place. As we sat on the porch of Neal's shop, the pups bounced off into the woods to put an invading squirrel in his proper place. They returned with a look of great satisfaction. Before I left that day, Boss and Sugar Bear had draped their lanky, muscular frames across my lap!

Old Things

I like old things. My rifles, save one 1874 Sharps and one 1885 Winchester high wall, are 18th Century style flintlocks. My bows are of wood.

Some would proffer that my affinity to the old is related to my own age. True, I am old, but I fail to see that as a qualifier regarding my propensity toward the antique. It all goes far deeper than mere years.

Each who falls victim to the lure of the ancient has his or her own reasons for the drive to explore those ages that came before. Perhaps it is simply curiosity. That is valid. A basic interest in how and why things were done is a solid draw, causing one to investigate. Or perhaps it is that and more.

Personally, I have contemplated my own journey into old things for many years. A long list of the whys surface, some obvious and some more apocalyptic. Pure pleasure is one of the more obvious. My old-style rifles and bows and canvas tents and buckskin leggings provide hours of enjoyment to life. I don't want to think of living without them.

Then there is the element of challenge, particularly when the use of such tools is associated with hunting and/or competition. Seems humanity is at its best when given a challenge that will require digging into the very depths of being to accomplish. Many will fail to see the benefits of such and attempt to avoid the rigors associated with it, but challenge is essential to growth.

And there is the opportunity to experience life as most of us in the modern world have never experienced it, if only briefly and in a pretend manner. To momentarily be whisked away from deadlines and demanding schedules and step into an era when time meant something different than it does now gives pause to wonder. We can wonder how well we would have done in this scheme of survival and providing shelter and finding sustenance. We can wonder if we would have been the successful predator or the captured prey. We can wonder about a great many things that come to mind when we enter a world apart from the day-to-day.

And we must not forget those factors that are not so easily defined, those things that pull and direct and coax us to dabble in antiquity. These can be complex, often even alarming. And they may best be described by the ambiguity of magic. There may be no definitive answers to those whys, and there may not need to be any answers. It can all be wrapped into that package of uncertainty. We do these things because we must, no additional reasons required.

In all this I have no contention with those who don't share my enthusiasm, particularly where hunting and shooting are concerned. They are free to employ technology as they wish. I must remember that what I use was once on the leading edge of technology. And finding fault with others or adopting some elitist persona can only lead to divisiveness. In a world that is so politically dangerous as the one in which we live, divisiveness is a nail in the coffin of the things so many of us hold dear. There are those who at best don't understand us and at worst actively seek to take away from us our most precious treasure – the freedom to enjoy and experience life as we choose to live it in conjunction with nature.

So, I will continue as best I can and as long as I can to embrace the days of those who came before me in the midst of the days and time I have been placed here and given. Those who don't, however, are missing out on a great deal. But then I like old things.

One Hunter's Journal

Day 1 – 6:00 a.m.: This is opening morning. I am sitting a stand located along an oak ridge just above a soybean field on the eastern edge of what we here in Mississippi call the Delta. The Delta is a broad expanse of flat, rich earth spreading over millions of acres along either side of the Mississippi River. These productive soils produce in abundance everything that grows here: crops, wildlife. If it will grow to outsized specifications, all it needs is a smile from nature and time to do that here. Quite spectacular, the Delta.

The sun is up, poking fingers of misty light through a canopy of leaves on an unseasonably cool morning for this area at this time – early October. Usually the mosquitoes are buzzing and sweat is trickling down my back when I sit here, but not today. It is glorious. The oaks are rattling in a tiny breeze, and leaves have already begun to lose their bright green. Reds and oranges are now replacing that color of summer. The honey locust pods have curled and begun to drop. One such tree is stationed just down the ridge from me; deer tracks surround it.

And over there a few yards, I hear a rustle. My heart quickens. I scan the surroundings for the source of that distinctive crunch that practically shouts, "deer!" A six point drifts up the slope, but his chosen route takes him 10 yards too far out for a reasonable shot. I relax the grip on a Flemish-twist string and watch in exhilaration. This is the first deer of a new season, and the importance of that can't be negated by the failure to get a shot. I smile.

The morning has some age now; nothing but squirrels moving. I opt to take a break back at camp, a simple set of two tents and a canvas awning erected for cooking. But simple is more than adequate. It is worlds apart from deadlines and laptops and ringing telephones. I need simple today.

3:30 p.m.: I am back on stand. Afternoons are often more fruitful than mornings in this particular spot. Deer leave thick tangles to the east and head westward toward the soybeans. My ridge is the last stop before they drop into that mystical flatness that goes on for miles to the Big Muddy. But it is not to be. Plenty of squirrels, again. But no whitetails. I leave as quietly as possible and switch on a small headlamp to help me navigate around the rattlers that, like the deer, grow big in these parts. I plan as I walk.

I will eat a light supper, sit by the campfire and watch stars dance, and then I will crawl into my sleeping bag early – by 9:00 p.m. at the latest. I will be serenaded by the haunting cries of coyotes and listen to the nighttime insects chirp and chatter until I drift off to comforting sleep, this world of wild things separated from me only by a thin fabric wall.

Day 2 – 6:00 a.m.: I am back where I was yesterday. Same tree. Looking for the same thing. Another pleasant morning, but the heat and humidity are not so agreeable as yesterday. This more accurately fits the norm but is not as inviting as the previous day's greeting. I daydream.

I think of that first archery deer. That was in 1973. No, it was 1974. Could it possibly have been that long? The buck was a three point – eastern count. He came from a pine plantation into some oaks en route to soybeans. The arrow intercepted him before he made that complete journey, and I sat beside him in awe. The sun cast its melancholy shadows about me as I did, and I was overcome with emotion, sentiment. My first archery deer. I concluded then that no other animal could mean as much, and the years have proven that conclusion reliable.

I think of what will likely be my one and only trip to Africa. I am sitting alone on a mountainside, stroking the rich coat and magnificent spiral horns of an Eastern Cape kudu bull. As per my request, the PH has left me behind while he goes to collect the truck a mile or so back. The PH is late; the sun is gone and the night has come. The PH, I later learn, high centered the truck on a rock. Rectifying that situation took him more than an hour – his cause for tardiness.

I hear the night sounds, sounds that are fully unfamiliar to a simple man from another continent. I stare at the Southern Cross, can almost reach up and feel the Milky Way as it brushes a transparent sky. I shiver in the chill. Or perhaps I shiver when pondering possible outcomes of this evening.

I consider the years, the experiences. These somehow meld into a blurred yet oddly identifiable catalog of individual events and times. Truck lights break my reverie. I am suddenly back in that stand on the oak ridge in Mississippi.

Nothing shows this morning. I head to camp.

3:30 p.m.: That stand again. The afternoon is uneventful. I leave a touch discouraged, but a fire and meal and warm sleeping bag will no doubt lift spirits. A weather front is forecast to move through. That should change the dynamics for tomorrow.

Day 3 – 5:45 a.m.: The wind is blowing. A thundercloud postures in the west; looks ominous. A crack of lightning in the distance dissuades me from continuing my vigil. I will ride out the inclement goings-on at camp.

4:00 p.m.: The storm is over. My boots are double size because of that Delta buckshot mud I contacted getting to this location that, by now, feels like home. My hopes are high and the safety harness is secured. I sit back and wait. And then those mental ramblings.

I realize with some trepidation that I am no longer that young bowhunter who took a three point in 1974. I am not even that adult who, several years back, sat on an African hillside and admired an incredible kudu. I don't climb trees or mountains with the same agility and abandon I once did. The joints creak and ache with monotonous regularity. Two have even called for surgery. Age is insistent, collecting its own sinister tariffs. I can't help but wonder how much longer I can participate in this activity that has been an integral part of my life, my being. I can't help but wonder what I will do and how I will react when the inevitable manages a firm grip and I have to admit that I can no longer continue. Sobering thoughts, these.

And then that familiar crunch in the leaves. And that unmistakable pop as a deer bites into an acorn. A bamboo-backed Osage bow comes up, a cedar shaft zips away, and a big Delta doe crashes just down the hill. The hunt is over. I will deal with those imagined prospects that occupied my mind minutes earlier at a later time.

2011: Reflections from the Past; Hope for the Future

This season seems to instigate a sequence of mental ramblings that touches a great many emotions. This, I suppose, comes from the fact that we have experienced the passing of a year – always a sobering realization. And we stand on the edge of another - an occasion that prompts us to dream and hope. This is as it should be, for the past can only be analyzed; it can't be altered. The future lies before us with few certainties, but it is at the moment here, to be dealt with as it unfolds. Much of what transpires will be beyond our control, but much will also be the direct result of our individual decisions. That too, like the passing mentioned above, is sobering. Choosing wisely is a prudent goal.

While taking apart 2010 in my mind, I find some elements of regret – both for things done and things not done. I regret not spending more time with my wooden bows on the target range and in the field. Such time soothes my entire being. But part of that lost time was the result of caregiving demands associated with aging parents. The chore was, often for weeks on end, an everyday requirement. But no regrets surface when I look back over these past 12 months as they relate to that particular part of life. What I did was what I should have done, what I must do. I will gladly do it again in 2011 if the need is there.

One outdoor endeavor that shines brightly in recall as I re-visit 2010 is a bison hunt in Kansas with Lee Hawes. Several years back, just on such a pivotal point as this new year upon which we now stand, I determined I wanted to hunt bison. Cowboy fashion. Horseback. Camps of tipis and dugouts. Meals from a Dutch oven. Stories of this era, filled with tragedy and waste but tempered with the eventual recovery of the bison, have always captured me.

But I didn't particularly want to hunt these magnificent be-ings with the bow and arrow. That in itself was a strange conclusion for me, but it was the Sharps rifle loaded with cast bullets and black powder cartridges that worked into my very core as the tool of choice for this hoped-for excursion. As I've just said, a strange con-clusion.

But no regrets. No regrets of taking the hunt or using the Sharps. No regrets of waking to the prairie wind whipping the smoke flaps of a tipi. No regrets of sitting by a quiet campfire as stars danced in a night sky above the Great Plains. No regrets of lying awake at night and listening to the coyotes cry from distant hillsides. No regrets of having shed quiet tears as I stroked the rich, thick mane of my bull bison as the sun lost altitude to a western horizon.

And there are other memories of the year just gone that conjure up no regrets: Gentle summer evenings spent constructing cedar arrows and trimming turkey-feather fletching; quiet morn-ings spent roaming woods and fields near home, Osage bow in hand; a simple tent camp not far from the Mississippi River, where whitetails came at dusk to visit the soybean fields; the familiar tug on a rope as a worthy companion and I extracted a downed deer from a tangle and transported this grand gift back to that camp; a campfire around which my wife and I sat and watched night age; family, both immediate and extended; and yes, even the caregiving. No regrets.

But what of this new year? Its offerings and perhaps obstacles remain anything but certain. But each will be there – offerings and obstacles. My hope is that some of the offerings afford a taunt bow string and the mystique of an arrow's flight. My hope is that I will not fail to grasp all this and let it sink into my soul. And my hope for the obstacles is that I handle them with gentleness, understanding, compassion. I would genuinely like to end this newest of the years I have been given with even fewer regrets than those of past years. I want to choose wisely.

Waiting for Ducks
in the Flooded Timber

I admit it: March is an unusual time for contemplating duck hunting. Duck season is over, and there is no chance of participating in this pursuit until a long summer is behind us and winter once again has North America in its grip. But please, I beg your indulgence.

Only a few days back as this is written, I went duck hunting. My only attempt this year. I didn't come away with birds for a cornbread dressing, but it was glorious just the same.

Duck hunting is a unique endeavor. It can be cold and wet and generally miserable, but it is enchanting just the same. Depending upon location, ducks can be hunted by various methods. There is river hunting; jump shooting around potholes; or decoying in sloughs, lakes, bays, or grain fields. Even hunting sea ducks. There is always variety. But if one persuasion were singled out as being classic duck hunting, particularly here in the Southeast, that would be hunting in flooded timber. This approach resonates with romance, mystique, the genteel of waterfowling.

And that is exactly what I did on this hunt – went to the flooded timber. The outing took place along the Noxubee River. This area is a jewel in the hunting world, with big bucks, wild hogs,

59

and turkeys in abundance. But it was the ducks in a riverside slough that captured my interest. The hunt gave me an opportunity to load up and tote my battered Browning A-5, another classic. That happens far too seldom for my liking.

Four hunters and a camera man slipped into waders and eased across a hardwood flat, hoping to gather footage for upcoming TV shows. The leaves were wet, so our approach was relatively quiet. When the slough came into view, we could see ducks – mallards, woodies. They were scattered in every direction and would have none of our intrusion. In flocks of five or six or 10 or two dozen, they burst from the water and shot skyward. We hoped some would return during legal shooting time. With stations selected, we waited.

Some did return. They streaked through the timber at full speed or glided high above in reconnaissance formation to get an overview of the situation. And even though they drew our attention, few afforded any viable shooting. The afternoon aged in a hasty fashion and someone called time. Legal shooting was over. Shotguns were unloaded. There was nothing left to do now but sit back and watch the grand spectacle of ducks at sunset.

And it was a grand spectacle. Eight mallards dropped from the sky and splashed into the slough. Then the gadwalls came. Perhaps a dozen. And over there, behind the trees and brush, more mallards. Twenty, maybe 30. A lone suzy offered her forlorn quack in the distance.

Then it was wood ducks. Ten in this flock; 25 over there; a half dozen to the right. They zipped by at tree-top height and made a wide circle. Three drakes, almost gaudy, backed their wings and disturbed the water's surface as they touched down. It was a color show unavailable outside the natural world.

And their calls! Much discussion can go into what makes a wild vocalization wild and which among the great collection of wild things and their sounds is indeed the wildest. Some might say the bugle of bull elk rises to the top of wildness. Some others might say the roar of an African lion wins the contest. And there are others who elect the turkey's gobble as a paramount player. I have heard them all and shuddered in excitement. But my vote goes to the wood duck. That plaintive, haunting, distant squeal can coax a smile from the most jaded and a shiver from the most stoic.

Perhaps one element that enhances the call of ducks is that it comes from beings that are not bound to Earth's floor. They have, under their own power given them by the Creator, the ability to fly. They have wings. They are able to soar above and see with ease from a perspective that the others can't even imagine. That is spectacular in and of itself.

As was this hunt. Spectacular. The fact that no birds came to bag was inconsequential.

Simple Therapy for the Tattered Spirit

Truth be known, we all probably need a little therapy now and again. Not therapy that focuses on strengthening repaired knees or stretched shoulders, though this is essential in various situations. The therapy we often need is that which weaves back into place spirits that have been tattered. This tattering can come quickly, as in times of sudden loss. But it can also creep in subtly after extended periods of excessive demands on our time and abilities. However it arrives, arrive it will.

While I didn't fully realize it then, I know now that I discovered in childhood a powerful entity that never failed to work its therapeutic magic. This marvelous little thing was a campfire, and its efficacy remains.

In those early years, a campfire was a near constant for country boys such as I. We camped regularly, perhaps two or three nights a week – out in the pasture or down by the creek after chores were completed in the afternoon. Simple affairs, these camps. More times than not just a quilt spread out on the ground. But there was always a campfire.

Let it be firmly established here that a fire is not some curious addition to an outdoor experience. It is mandatory, vital. True, there are times when a fire is not permitted because of prevailing restraints, but if these are not factors a fire simply must be. It becomes the centerpiece, not an ornament. Why? That likely varies from individual to individual, from circumstance to circumstance.

A campfire – even if there is no literal camp – is the point of gathering. Participants yield to its lure. Someone may do a bit of rudimentary cooking, but more than likely everyone will just sit and stare, those stares broken by jovial or somber conversation. There will be laughter, perhaps even tears.

Sitting around a campfire permits one to become transformed, almost as if the world outside that gentle glow of light does not exist. Maybe that is the primary therapeutic element, this transformation that for the moment shuts out all else and bandages those ragged edges of the heart so that they may more quickly heal.

A campfire's coals are mesmerizing. Their enchantment allows the silent observer to probe distant depths of his or her mind, depths that are seldom explored. Those varying hues of orange, blue, yellow; that little spot that jets flame out to the side; the hiss and crackle; an orchestrated yet spontaneous dance; the warmth on your face that at times approaches too much but pulls you close just the same: All are present there in the coals. All are hypnotic. All are healing.

The smell: It is unmistakable. The modern world may tell us to avoid such odors as those emitted by a campfire. And perhaps these are ill placed if we are dressed for the office or business conference. But taken for what it is and in its proper setting, the smell of a campfire is a primal badge of honor. There was a time in the not-too-distant history of humanity when that smell meant comfort, safety. My perspective is that it still does. The smell represents a basic ingredient for life and should not be dismissed as antiquated.

And consider the process of a campfire. It mimics life. One

form of matter is placed onto the coals to be in large measure used up, to provide its heat and light. Another form of that matter is not consumed and spirals skyward toward freedom. That in itself prompts contemplation. And all these can be found in a campfire.

September: Sound and Sensibility

My apologies to novelist Jane Austen for being perilously close to plagiarism in that title. But this is September, and it is a month filled with sound and sensibility. While the weather likely remains hot and somewhat disagreeable in the South, this time of year is particularly palatable. In short, September is spectacular.

September is a turning point in seasons. The Autumnal Equinox comes near the close of this month; it is that spot on the calendar marking the end of summer and the beginning of fall. That one day will see daylight and dark of even measure, but from then forward the days will progressively shorten. Dusk will soon ride on the coattails of 5:00 p.m. But we must remember that though September is the harbinger of cold and damp, it does not allow us to be held captive in winter's grip just yet. That is cause for celebration.

And what of those sounds and sensibilities? They are too numerous to list.

The careful eye has already begun to notice a curious slant to afternoon shadows. That glare of summer is gone, replaced by some soft, feathery whisper of gentleness as the sun casts its light in a less obtrusive manner. Gentleness is a good thing. And such scenes as are presented on a September afternoon, if we will allow, prepare us for reflection, give us the opportunity to come to know ourselves better.

And the skies are azure – deep and distant and haunting in a pleasant sort of way. They summon, call us outside ourselves. We can, on a September sunrise, see wisps of clouds against that grandest of skies as these ribbons of mist appear to be drawn toward that sun. And we can permit ourselves, at least in our imagination, to drift in that direction as well, soaring above and away from the trappings that bind us, reaching for insights we have never before grasped. We can fly after all!

Keep watch on the leaves. They are not yet in their full autumn garb, but they are making ready. Perhaps the black gum now wears red to accentuate its green. The hickory may show some tints of yellow. Before long they will all be at their finest, and that finest is truly breathtaking.

The sweet gum, lowly and common and disfavored, can cast a spell. One yellow or brown leaf can dangle at one particular angle and catch the slightest breeze. That leaf will dance with the wind and bump others of its kind. The sound is a soft ticking, not really music but not far from it. Sit and observe that leaf at length. Move from yourself and become that leaf. Consider who may have seen and heard such in the past; imagine who will have or seize the same opportunity in the future.

Much the same can be said for corn stalks in a secluded field. The leaves have served their primary purpose and have crinkled and withered and twisted, but they now serve a secondary and most important purpose of telling stories of life as they rustle to and fro. Listen carefully; they will speak.

And probably in that same field the insects will sing – crickets, grasshoppers, katydids. Their drones are long and mournful; however, they are peaceful. And these may be accompanied by the caw of a crow or the hoot of an owl or the chatter of a jay. This is life – apart from our own but life just the same. Consider it all.

There could be geese, these proffering a haunting song drifting from above and in the distance. Where they have come from and where they are going is a guess at best. But they travel the path that their inner directives tell them to travel. As their kind has done for hundreds of years. Heard on an autumn day, it is a melancholy symphony of wildness that somehow touches the very core of one who encounters and contemplates such a melody.

And suppose you go and there are none of these sounds. What then? Listen instead to the quiet. It will be abundant. Far too few are the opportunities to listen to quiet in today's world. September is the perfect month for it all.

Bull Moose and the Splat of Snowflakes

After our Super Cub disappeared around the mountains and the drone of its engine faded, there was only silence. That is not a bad thing, for there is too little silence in this world of boisterous and disruptive noise.

But then again, it was not silence if this were measured by the absence of sound. Sound was abundant: The repetitive splat of snowflakes; that gurgling rush of the Graham River pouring over bathed stones honed smooth by the flow; the rumble of wind drifting from cathedral slopes and then morphing to a haunting moan in the alders near camp; the shrill call of an eagle; an occasional and mystifying howl of a wolf. No, silence was not there. Only the absence of those mundane and spirit-robbing rackets with which most of us are too familiar.

An hour or so before, my writer friend Bryce Towsley and I had arrived at a quaint ranch house tucked deeply into the wilderness of British Columbia. The trip there, after the initial flights on commercial jets, had necessitated a 90-mile drive up the Alaska Highway, followed by a 40-mile jump in the first Super Cub. Gear off loaded there at the ranch, headquarters for this hunt, we poked individual belongings into a second single engine and went to base

camp, one hunter at a time, some 30 miles upriver. I won the toss
to go first; Bryce would follow directly if daylight and weather allowed. If not, I would have that secreted-away camp to myself until
the next morning.

I admit to a bout with trepidation. Spending a night alone
in such a distant and possibly dangerous setting was bothersome.
"Watch out for the grizzlies," Darwin had shouted above the rumble of the plane as he slammed that fragile two-piece door shut and
roared down a snow-dusted runway cut with a chainsaw from an
old burn. I quickly busied myself at stowing gear in one of two low-
slung log huts, rifle close at hand. But honesty forces me to pro-
claim that I breathed a sigh of relief to hear that bumblebee sound
emitting from a far-off speck as Darwin delivered my companion
just before nightfall. All was well, and when everyone was assem-
bled the following day, we would begin a moose hunt.

Moose are the largest member of the deer family. Depending upon the subspecies and habitat, the weight of a given bull can
go well above 1,000 pounds. Height at the shoulders can rise to
seven feet. By any standards these are huge animals. And this was
the first time that any of us would have the possibility of collecting
a moose. The meat is quite grand, and hopes ran high that we
would leave camp, the plane loaded with back straps and steaks and
antlers. Only time would reveal the integrity of those hopes.

Daylight the first morning found us stumbling around and
heading to the cook shack. A huge breakfast greeted us, as did the
guides. The wranglers were sorting tack and making horses ready
for a long ride into the mountains. Those mountains, encircling
camp in a white coat that glistened in morning sun, towered above
and proffered both an invitation and warning. This was gloriously
magnificent and judiciously threatening country that was not to be
taken for granted. We soon stepped into stirrups and slumped into
saddles, our shoulders bent and hats pulled low against a ferocious
wind on which rode a chill that can only be generated in some wild

and snow-covered environ. The hunt had begun.

Not far from camp, miles away from our planned destination up near Laurier Pass, we saw moose. A cow or two here; a young bull sparring with another his size there. The cold forgotten for a moment, we sat and stared. Being in the company of these grandiose wild things was an uncommon pleasure. But it was time to climb higher, so we nudged the horses forward to the squeak of saddle leather and that fluttering snort that horses emit. The world was alive with galvanizing excitement.

At somewhere near 6,000 feet of elevation, we stopped and took the spotting scope from a saddle bag. With it positioned on a short tripod, we sat and glassed everything for a mile around. Over there, to the north, a peak rose abruptly from a narrow valley, and half-way up that peak were black specks in short brush. Moose! A closer look through powerful glass showed that one was a big bull, a bull with an unusual antler configuration. Rather than the wide span most often encountered, this one's antlers went out and turned at almost a 90-degree angle upward. The points coming off the main beams down near the bull's head were spectacular – perhaps as big around as my forearm and elbow-to-fingertips long. Three on one side; two on the other. We elected to try for this bull.

The plan was simple. We would ride the horses through the valley below and up the mountainside in hopes of locating the bull. One specific rock and brush cluster was our targeted locale. But we met with disappointment. Before we arrived at our station, we bumped the bull and he tore through the brush with an agility and pace that belied his size and cumbersome appearance. That hunt ended with too little daylight remaining for another try. It was time to head for camp.

I have had only limited experience with horses. I owned one when I was young, but the riding of that animal was confined to jaunts around an 80-acre farm we called home. The use of them as viable and essential transportation in such remoteness was for-

eign to me. And riding minus light in grizzly country was truly unnerving. But Sandy, our guide, gave basic instruction that proved reliable. Sandy was a member of a local Indian tribe and knew these
mountains well. "Get on and stay on!" he admonished. Conversation was not high on his already skeletal list of social graces.
That ride was incredible even though it held us in its Gothic grip.
Darkness swallowed us quickly, as it does in high mountains.

Horses plodded along, alder branches tugging at stirrups
and boots, spruce limbs slapping faces and hats. Save that phantom-like moan of wind and the occasional click of metal shoes on
rocks, there were no sounds. Human speech seemed completely out
of place.

In such settings the mind can play sinister tricks. Out there,
somewhere in the inky nothingness, were grizzlies. That crunch in
the brush can easily convince one that an attack is imminent. The
jerking to attention of the head by a docile mount can send shivers
of carnage up the rider's spine. A tensing of muscles and the slightest hesitation on the horse's part can cause one to claw with icy fingers at the rifle scabbard. And not unlike Dorothy in "The Wizard
of Oz," who allowed that she was no longer in Kansas, I was absolutely certain that I was no longer in Mississippi – or anywhere
else I had ever been.

Then, Aurora Borealis rescued me. Colors danced and
darted across a sky filled with stars and gave pause to look upward
toward the light rather than downward into darkness. And now,
some five miles later in the saddle amidst haunting uncertainties,
more light was added. In the distance two gas lanterns flickered
outside warm huts near the river.

The next day was one that turned out difficult to describe.
We left camp in a heavy drizzle that soaked our wool without hesitation. But climbing higher put us above the rain. Up there, with
the valley hundreds of feet below, there was snow. It drifted down
gently at first, but then it blew horizontally, riding powerful gusts
that numbed exposed skin and coaxed us to seek relief in heavy

coats. We were headed to hundred-moose valley, so named because Darwin noted that about this time each year there may be as many as 100 animals collected in that little mountain bowl. And there were, maybe not 100 but quite a few. We spoiled one stalk and found nothing else of great interest. We elected to move on. The move, however, was barely begun when we saw a herd of mountain caribou. Grand animals, and we watched for several minutes.

On down a bit farther were three white dots high on top and made visible only because the snow was even whiter. Mountain goats. Another first for Bryce and me. Sandy urged us on.

And then a serendipity that we had hardly considered possible. Scattered along a skinny ledge just short of a mountain crest were Stone's sheep. A herd of ewes and lambs and a small collection of young rams to the right. To the left were three more, bedded and content. Bryce and I extracted a binocular and spotting scope and had our first visual on mature rams, all full curl. Magnificent. We wished to stay there and soak in this fragile and fleeting gift, but Sandy grunted and in near staccato fashion managed the words, "Let's go." He led us to a spot for which no descriptors are adequate.

"Indians hunted here," he said as we stepped from the saddles. "Some died here." Above this secretive and haunting huddle of aspens and boulders, a stream poured over the peak, its cascading roar ending in a tiny pool and stream hundreds of feet below. The place was appealing, but there was something about it that prompted anxiety. We attempted to start a fire and warm as we ate lunch. The fire failed.

Now, none of us were inexperienced in the art of fire building. We could accomplish the task with modern matches or lighters, or we could manage it with flint and steel and char. Starting a fire was nothing other than common. Except here. The initial lighting would blaze up, only to fade immediately into a cold void of wispy smoke. I had that confusing feeling of not being welcome all the while we ate sandwiches and drank cold mountain water straight from the stream. Even Sandy exhibited some recognizable degree of angst. Without addressing the situation, he began stuffing his lunch container into a saddle bag and suggested we ride back down and look for moose.

Perhaps you will recall that back a few paragraphs where I began this portion of the story, I indicated that this day would turn out to be one difficult to describe. It was. How do you describe the surreal? How do you talk with conviction and validity about haunted places, spirit beings? How does modern, educated, and so-phisticated man struggle with the possibility of ghosts? I don't know. But I do know that Bryce and I were yet uneasy even after we tucked into sleeping bags later that night. This particular spot of majestic landscape that looked down on camp from miles away was filled with something neither he nor I had known. As wolves howled in the distance, we concurred that something was amiss. Haunting, it was.

The next day put us in our only close contact with the most formidable beast of this high country – the grizzly. As we rode a rocky trail through big timber, one particular spot grabbed our at-tention. A grizzly track, still soft in the mud and still filling with water that was oozing from the melting snow that the bear's weight had pushed aside. Bryce and I dismounted to get a better look, all the while scanning the shaded and shadowed surroundings for any threat. I placed my gloved hand, fingers spread widely, and a .35 Whelen cartridge in the track as Towsley snapped a photo. There was ample track backward, forward and on each side of the car-tridge and hand. A sobering thought – the mental vision of this great bear.

Still, we had not seen a grizzly. That, however, was about to change!

Sandy urged us on from the photo episode at the track with some gruff grunts and anxious coaxing to move along. As we followed he mentioned something about an old moose kill he knew of over the next rise. Some grizzly or a cruel twist of weather had claimed another animal, and the bears were making good use of the remains. We needed to navigate precariously close to that very spot while en route to another area. Anxiety rose to another level.

As we broke over the crest overlooking the carcass, a silver-backed grizzly rose on hind legs and stared. Off to the side a duet of young, probably this big sow's cubs and each weighing perhaps 200 pounds, danced about in excitement at the intrusion. The horses commenced snorting and bouncing and preparing for evacuation. The sow swayed from side to side, popping her teeth and offering a bluff charge as time moved into slow motion and our reflexes froze as solidly and stiffly as the high-land puddles. It was is if we were unattached from the situation and simply silent observers stationed off in the distance, safely watching a magical and mystical video of nature in its most natural. Truth was, however, we were in grave danger.

Fast forward and the unscheduled encounter ended without incident. The sow dropped to all fours and ambled away, her silver back undulating in sunlight and her cubs in tow. A display as keen in memory today as it was more than a decade ago when it occurred. For the remainder of that day the horses shied from every shadow and refused to walk near dark timber around the edges of openings. They snorted and perked their ears in various directions, no doubt detecting the noxious smell of bears. Back at camp, all was peaceful.

Our hunt was winding down. It seemed we had been there only two days, when in fact we had completed five. The next we left camp more determined than ever. And that determination produced its reward with Towsley's bull. He took the animal from a distant slope with one well-placed shot from his .375 H&H. The bulk of the following day was given over to packing out meat and antlers. Then it was my turn.

We found that unusual bull of the second day, again in the same spot we had found him earlier. This time, however, we employed a more secretive approach. We tied the horses in the valley and climbed quietly for perhaps two hours to reach the brush where the bull and three cows were located. It was time to collect my moose.

An aside here: I was fortunate to consider checking my rifle before the climb. We had been in rain and snow all the way up, and I was curious about the condition of the rifle's action. Rounds were in the magazine but not in the chamber. I attempted to open the bolt. It refused. Frozen solidly shut. I had to use the heel of my boot to get it loose, and then on an empty chamber I tried the trigger and firing pin. The pin would not fall. In a makeshift effort to rectify the action's frigid posture, I removed the bolt and dropped it inside the many layers of wool I wore. Its chill caused me to gasp as it slid into place just above my belt. It was here that the bolt resided during the climb. The body warmth, I hoped, would thaw the mechanism.

It did! When I loaded again before the final approach, the firing pin snapped pleasingly in an empty chamber. And then we were there, that big bull standing less than 100 yards away. The rumble of my .35 and the bullet's whump announced a climatic finish to this hunt. And once again, God's magnificent creation had given me far more than I deserved. Not only did I have a moose, but I had a collection of experiences and memories that I have brought to recall practically every day since. And all are as filled with wonderment as was that mysterious and far-off land and uncommon creatures that call it home.

The Grandest of Seasons

Perception is powerful. Something that is treasured by one can be minus value to another. So at the risk of ascribing tremendous worth to an entity that may not hold the same for someone else, I advance my perception: Autumn is the grandest of seasons!

Since perception plays a key role here, it is permissible and advisable to recognize how and why that perception was shaped. I speak only for myself when I say autumn heralded the beginning of a great many things I held dear in childhood and youth. That has not changed.

The rural Southeast U.S. was, in my childhood and again now in later years, home. Life as a child, now 50 years in the past, was basic: Heavy farm work, few amenities, simple pleasures. And while much of this remained unchanged regardless of season, those arduous farm chores were accentuated in spring and summer. Then came autumn, a welcomed metamorphosis.

Autumn loosed the grip of sweltering heat and humidity. It broke the mundaneness of plowing and hoeing. It afforded an opportunity, at least in our tiny world, to slow, to relax to some degree. It brought a beauty unlike any other.

Those old sweet gum trees employed a few weeks prior as shade under which vegetables were cleaned and prepared for canning became a rare portrait, their yellow and gold and orange leaves sparkling in the autumn sunshine. Corn stalks, their ears now gathered and put away, were austere. But even they produced an element of magic as their withered arms rustled a quaint and mysterious song when disturbed by an autumn breeze already holding the hint of chill.

The cotton bolls were empty. But the fruit they had held provided opportunity for one of life's greatest pleasures. Nothing is as sweet smelling and gentle feeling as a wagon load of hand-picked cotton warmed in the autumn sun.

But perhaps the most memorable and the one thing that most shaped my life was the fact that autumn spelled the beginning of hunting season. Somewhat different now than then, this was a time to gather foods other than those grown on the farm. Mostly squirrels and rabbits and quail. The occasional duck. Deer in our area were only a distant promise. But those early experiences pointed me to a life in the outdoors, and that hope for the now ubiquitous whitetail caught a spark then that never dimmed. I fully recall that first time I climbed a tree, stickbow in hand, and had deer materialize before me. The cedar arrow chattered on the rest and never experienced flight from my bow. But no matter; I had seen deer.

All these things and more are affiliated with autumn. These shaped my perception of the season and still have a firm grip on my very core. And that time, autumn, is here, at least here in the Southeast U.S. – my home. Now is without question the grandest of seasons!

Ramblings of an Antique

Call me an antique. To that designation I nod in deference and plead guilty. For I am an antique – both in practice and sentiment.

My bows are bamboo and Osage; my arrows cedar. My muzzleloader is a Lancaster-style flintlock. My modern center fire is an 1874 Sharps, its thumb-sized brass cases stuffed with black powder and topped with lead slugs. And to add credence to this reference of antiquity, I began regular treks into the hunting woods in the late 1950s. Seems everything I am and know and possess and use is old.

But save age, over which I have no control, all other ingredients that relate to practice, and to sentiment I suppose, are a matter of choice. There is pure magic in the feel and cast of a wooden bow. There is a euphoric aroma that rises toward heaven during the processing of a cedar shaft. There is romance in the clack, whoosh, boom of a flintlock. There is nostalgic mystique in the rumble of a black-powder cartridge. No other contrivances of humanity with which I am acquainted have so completely locked me into their unyielding spell as have those just mentioned. As a result, I practice the old. Always will.

That practice often generates comment when I am in new company. Questions are common, all of which I am more than happy to answer if I possibly can. And there is often a quiet hint of interest that emerges, giving promise that another individual has allowed an embryo of intrigue to enter some deep spot inside. It may grow to maturity in the future. But seldom during any of these interactions is there one who takes offense to my mode of operation. That is as long as I keep my proclivity for strong sentiment under control. It is this element that is most likely to put me in opposition to some of the more modern among the hunting fraternity.

Sentiment causes me to struggle with many terms and behaviors now common in the hunting world. For instance, I wrestle with the nomenclature cull buck. I do support wildlife management and fully understand the concept of removing specific animals from a herd, but cull, at least in my aging mind, carries the connotation of insignificance. There is no buck, no animal in fact, that is insignificant. All are important, of value.

I have difficulty with high fives and fist bumping and similar displays of gleeful abandon at the taking of an animal. There is joy and a sense of satisfaction and accomplishment to be sure, but there is also an ample supply of sobering sadness, enough in fact to reign in rambunctious frivolity in favor of quiet reverence. An animal, any animal deserves nothing less.

Then there is the bad-boy, tough-guy, going-to-war approach. My dad's generation faced battle in World War II. My generation faced battle in Vietnam. Many others have faced battle since in other venues and there will be more in the future. These did and will indeed go to war. But it was not and will not be that outing in the deer woods.

Much thought and great care should also figure into the equation before hunting is viewed as a form of competition. Ill placed, it seems, is the thought of always having to win, whether with the animal or fellow hunters. It is natural and productive to have a deer or other game animal slip away, the beneficiary of keen senses and instinct. And the drive to always take the biggest or most seems a sinister demon that can rob a hunter of the true essence afforded by the experience.

I say none of this to take away from those with a different persuasion. There is room for difference. But for me, I will keep mine on a level at which I find the reward I seek, and that is to use tools of the past and relish in the simple pleasures of a grand and glorious creation, a creation I have celebrated now for more years than it seems possible. These are just my leanings when I consider the situation.

So please, feel free to call me an antique!

Romance Rekindled

"What happened to the romance?" Mike Yancey asked that question somewhere in Oklahoma as he and I were driving to Texas. The object of the trip was hog hunting and perhaps a chance encounter with a whitetail. We had been discussing the state of hunting and its related changes over the past two decades or so.

While I had never asked that question, at least audibly, I had pondered the concept and had even used that mystical word romance in various magazine articles and columns over the years. For you see, hunting has always been a romantic pursuit for me. And apparently the same was true for Yancey. We talked on a bit about this subject.

To understand it better, some viable definition of romance must be contrived. However, I am not sure that can be done with any degree of accuracy, for it would certainly vary from individual to individual. I can speak only for myself – and for Yancey in some measure as per his injections of wisdom into the conversation.

Hunting, even early on for me, meant some mysterious pursuit that was apart from anything else in my experiences. I enjoyed playing baseball, but it never possessed that phantom-like allure that hunting held. Hunting captured me, kept me in its clutches to the point that I dreamed about it. I made plans for grand travels and serendipitous exposures to terrific and unfamiliar wildlife and environs even though I had no regimen that would put me in any locale save the river swamp near home. But dreams were adequate at the time; they failed to fade. I was filled with the mystery of it all, the romance if you will. Yancey concurred.

There was also this deep and somewhat unrecognizable sensation of fulfillment associated with hunting. It seemed to center around self-sufficiency and the knowing that what I had done was not purely recreational. I came to this conclusion during the last game of the season when I caught a fly ball in the final inning, retiring the other team and giving us the championship. I was happy, excited, but that sensation of fulfillment melted away rather quickly.

Not so with hunting. The discipline required to locate and take game was something more than a cheering crowd under the lights of a small-town park and the smack of a fly ball in a tattered glove. That was a pleasant but momentary burst of exhilaration. Hunting was full of life lessons, its fulfillment remaining even today, its romance thoroughly real. Difficult or impossible to explain, but real just the same.

Yancey's initial question still directing the conversation, talk turned to what we see so often today and promoted as hunting. Perhaps it is; perhaps it isn't. Let me qualify my position on this by saying that I am aging; I am of the old school. So, I find it problematic to comprehend how such activity as I sometimes see can hold any semblance of romance. The gadgets and frivolity and what appears useless and even foolish attempts at humor. Standing precariously close to the precipice edge of disrespect for the animals pursued. Expecting, often demanding, the hunt to be immediate so that time remains for some additional endeavor or transport or visual entertainment. Indeed, what happened to the romance?

And what of our hog hunt? Successful. Additionally, we took hogs. Success does not necessitate taking game. Yancey, I am sure, experienced romance during his stalk and shot that resulted in a hog. And I? Romance blossomed with the arrow's flight and its true path. And although this mysterious, fulfilling element of true hunting did not need any such adjustment, romance was rekindled on that Texas hunt.

The Hunter's Dreams

Dreams are often strange experiences. Some may trouble peaceful sleep, while others are far more pleasant, even entertaining. It is these pleasant ramblings of the brain that we all hope for, not those that disturb or produce anxiety. The hunter's subconscious is filled with dreams – the pleasant ones anyway.

The older I get the more I realize that dreams make up a viable portion of the hunting life. Some, and perhaps the most important of this surreal world of dreaming, may occur minus sleep. Known commonly as daydreams, these creep into the everyday. Whether in the form of simple anticipation or in the realm of planning and imagining what the hunt will be like, they play a significant role in the enjoyment. In fact, they become a part of that enjoyment. Looking forward to something is always an exercise in mystique, in wonderment.

I recall as a young hunter those Saturday mornings with my dad in the squirrel woods. Small game was the extent of hunting to which we had access, and it was these small creatures that put me on track as a hunter. It was these that honed my skills and taught me respect for the game and my fellow hunters. It was these that filled our dinner table several times a week and provided food in some rather austere times. I am grateful to them all. And it was the trips in search of these that filled my dreams.

The pleasant malady of daydreams and sleep dreams never failed to afflict me no later than Thursday. That day signaled the approaching close of a work week for my dad and a school week for me. I was a high-school band member, and Friday nights were given over to half-time shows at football games in the fall, the season that overlapped squirrel season. I would begin on Thursday dreaming of and planning for that Saturday hunt, a hunt that would take place regardless of the late hour we returned from those away games that made up perhaps half the football schedule. Circumstances permitting, the squirrel hunt was a given. And oh the pleasant dreams it produced!

Time changes all things, as most of us have come to realize, but the dreams continue – both day and night. I am now dreaming in restful slumber of Texas turkeys. The hunt is only three weeks away as I write this. Thunderous gobbles drifting over prickly pear and through mesquite creep into quiet sleep; I wake with a smile and expectation. The following morning I abandon magazine deadlines to practice shooting seated from a blind, taking care to place cedar shafts properly from broadside and back. I sit and twist a new string when I should be completing another chapter of an upcoming book. I trim primary feathers to prescribed proportions when I should be developing another article. I opt for daydreaming rather than regimen.

And there is the kudu hunt, less than three months off at this point. Dreams have begun. I see that double helix rising over sage and thornbush, the bull carrying those spiraling horns treading silently and effortlessly through South Africa's red soil. I dream of him approaching my hide and stopping to stare in my direction. I envision him turning his head away and permitting a chance to bring the Osage to full draw. I see a heavy wood shaft and wide two-blade fly straight and true. Sleep is accompanied by shudders of excitement as I dream of walking up to a fallen monarch and kneeling in respect and thanksgiving. All these occur in my dreams

– those dreams during sleep as well as those during daytime awareness. Grand they are.

We hunters should never dismiss our dreams, in whatever
form they come. Rather, we should entertain them, embrace them.
They are, after all, an integral part of the enjoyment. They enhance
our lives. Dream well fellow hunters!

Passing It On and
Offering Instruction

"How do you shoot?" I had just handed the young man an extra Osage and bamboo bow from my rack and told him to keep it as long as he wanted. The youngster, I'd say 15, practices martial arts at the same dojo as I, and he frequently asks me about primitive and traditional archery. I always try to oblige.

This young man has the makings of an outstanding individual. Gentle, kind, well mannered, intelligent, a thirst for learning – he receives my vote. And he now holds the same rank in karate as I. Depending upon one's perspective, that speaks well of him or poorly of me. I have years of training on him, though interrupted. His high kick is a thing of beauty. It soars head high with ferocious speed. But then, so does mine. However, mine must first go to the knee, thereby rendering the opponent supine before loftier locales become viable targets! All this aside, however, I regretted his asking that question.

Truthfully, I don't know how I shoot. I long ago concluded that the system is some blend of a great many others and has morphed over the years into what some consider a distorted regimen that can't be accurately named. I greatly admire those who are pure instinct shooters. One such is a regular companion who executes a graceful push/pull as the bow swings from his side and on target.

As quickly as he touches anchor, the arrow is on its way. And in the game fields, he is as certain as anyone I have ever seen shoot. His system doesn't work for me.

And I have even received instruction from one who shot for some time with Howard Hill. This man who gave me that instruction talked about a secondary point of aim and how he got on target by this method. And get on target he did. Paper plates thrown into the air, golf balls bounced along the ground, squirrels or rabbits or deer – the arrow always connected. It took me two months after that to get back consistently into a 12-inch circle at 20 yards. His system doesn't work for me.

There is another shooter with whom I am acquainted who shoots what he says is the gap. He draws his bow and anchors with it perpendicular to the ground, and then holds and holds and holds. He can hit a tiny spot within a tiny spot. His system doesn't work for me.

And there is shaft shooting and three fingers under and nock to the eye and a broad host of others. These systems don't work for me.

I attempted to explain to the young man and address his question. "I put my bow arm out with the bow at about a 45-degree angle; I think I see the arrow tip in my peripheral vision but I'm not sure. Then I pull the string to full draw and middle-finger anchor tightly in the corner of my mouth and then form an imaginary line from my elbow down through the fingers and arrow and through the air to the target. And then I tilt my head hard into the string and make sure nothing is wobbling and let the arrow slip from my fingers almost by surprise. And I hold right there in that position until the arrow arrives. That's how I do it."

The young man listened intently and looked on in obvious confusion. He nodded. I then realized that whatever pedagogic skills I possessed in the exegesis of literature had likely stayed in the classroom at my retirement and clearly didn't transfer to explaining archery, at least not in this particular exchange. I finally told him that I was not at all certain that how he did it was of much importance as long as he had a well-developed and consistent anchor and smooth release and rock-solid follow through and that it worked for him.

"All I know as an absolute in my shooting," I said in conclusion, "is that when I do it right I hit and when I do it wrong I miss. The arrow goes every time exactly where I tell it to go." This he grasped fully. He smiled.

I then asked him how he did that marvelous high kick. "Nothing to it," he noted. He is too much the gentle sort to remind me that I am older than his grandfather!

Resolutions Bring Pause for Deeper Thought

A few days back as this is written, I went behind my house and climbed a tree stand for an afternoon hunt. Well, I was not really hunting; I was just out there thinking and enjoying the sleek lines and meticulous craftsmanship of one of my old rifles, an 1885 Winchester High Wall. I could see my house, a wisp of smoke curling from the chimney, two dogs puttering and lounging about the yard. The neighbor's car crunched along a gravel driveway. Traffic buzzed on a busy road just to the north. The day was January 1, 2011, and that fact prompted the practice that many of us engage in around this time every year – resolutions. I had made none to date, so I took this opportunity to rectify the situation.

I resolved to have more outdoor experiences in 2011 than I did in 2010. Taking this list on a seasonal basis, I resolved to hear the gobbles and see the gaudy displays of strutting turkeys. An incredible aural and visual performance, this. I resolved to visit a bream bed, antique bamboo flyrod in hand, and pull a belligerent bluegill from the water, the fish attracted by and attached to a tiny popping bug that had only seconds earlier been laid gently on the surface of a quiet lake. And while it is not specifically outdoors related, I resolved to make my kata more proficient and earn another belt in karate. After all, I was, even there in the stand, munching the last of what must have been 27 pounds of peanut brittle I had on hand for the holidays. The exercise involved in accomplishing this goal might help alleviate that pinch I was feeling at the waist of my blue jeans.

I resolved to see rainbow trout rise to a dry fly, preferably in Wyoming. Speak of magic and romance! Few things compare. I resolved to absorb the grace of my canoe guided silently over a secluded lake or down a placid stream. Maybe even feel again the rush of that same craft bobbing through crashing whitewater. I resolved to sleep more nights in a tent, the natural world only inches from my head.

I resolved to spend more spring and summer afternoons shooting my Sharps rifle, seeing that blue/grey puff of smoke from a charge of black powder and hearing the clank of hand-cast lead bullets smacking steel targets downrange at 200 yards. This keeps my spirit soaring and my imagination active.

I resolved to see more sunrises. Those in the spring would be accompanied by sweet smells, emerging leaves, blooming flowers, chattering squirrels, chirping birds darting here and there, and new grass decorating itself with a luxurious green coat that invites one to sit there and listen intently. Those sunrises of summer would shine through water droplets dripping from an extensive collection of vegetation. And autumn sunrises: They would be enchanting, haunting as they streak through a distant sky of azure and orange. In winter these sunrises would lie deeper to the south, bringing promise of easing the chill that would bite fingers and toes.

I resolved to marvel at the arc of a cedar arrow cast from a longbow. I resolved to recapture childhood as I watched a squirrel scurry up an oak and pluck an acorn for breakfast. I resolved to hear an elk bugle, to see a pronghorn buck herd his does in sagebrush prairie. I resolved to play in the snow, even if it meant going somewhere outside Leake County, Mississippi. I resolved, right here at home, to watch a whitetail tip from a thicket and nibble about the forest floor.

And then it happened. Just as I completed that resolution, a doe eased up the hill and toward my stand. Ending the drama would have been simple. The High Wall was positioned perfectly. But I was not really hunting. I smiled and continued with the resolutions. It was then that I came to a sobering realization.

None of the things I had just resolved and hoped to do were inherently evil. To the contrary; they would be beneficial to my wellbeing. But they were all focused on me, what I wanted and needed. It was then that I shifted direction in my resolving for the New Year.

I resolved to be more available to those who need me. I resolved to be a better and more concerned listener. I resolved to be quicker with a compliment, a word of encouragement, a thank you. To be more compassionate. And I resolved to more readily express my love. These latter resolutions are worth keeping.

Classics

I dearly love classic firearms. That word classic is perhaps a bit ambiguous if one were forced to present an accurate definition, and it can be applied in error if not fully understood. According to Webster, one applicable definition for the word as it is used here is: Famous or well known, especially as being traditional or typical. So in that context, I must say again that I dearly love classic firearms.

Most of the classic firearms to which I gravitate have, as many other classic items, fallen victim to advertised progress. Something new, something different, and something promoted as superior took the place of those classics, making the old ones difficult to find and/or priced out of the range of most of us. There are, however, a very few that are still made in almost perfect function and resemblance to the originals, but even these are generally expensive.

I have been fortunate over the years to own several guns that are now deemed classics. Some of the old used rigs available during my childhood are now classics. They would show up on racks in hardware stores as a result of a trade for the new and better units of the day, and they could be had for a song. But back then few of us could sing! Still, I managed to swap around and get something of interest from time to time. I didn't know it then; the trades and dealings were my own effort to move up in modernity.

I recall one deal my dad and I made. The result was that I took home a Winchester Model 12. It was then just a well-used but solid shotgun that offered more firepower than did my single barrel that went toward the trade. Today, it is a classic. Problem is, I traded it for something newer and better, never suspecting what I was doing. I still dream of that Model 12.

And there was a Remington auto; I believe it was the Model 11. Set up on that famous hump-back design of John Browning, it had the safety in front of the trigger in the guard housing. Perfect for a left hander such as I. And a real shooter, too. I took squirrels, rabbits, quail, and ducks with that 12 gauge, again never grasping the fact that I was then toting around what would become a classic. And like the Model 12, I traded it.

In a move that later proved wise, I kept poking around the local Western Auto store and admiring the Browning A-5s on the rack there. I agonized over them, trying always to determine which gauge and choke configuration I would get when I was able to acquire one. I talked this over with my dad, and he agreed to go with me and sign a note that I might purchase the A-5. The payments were $25.00 a month if I recall, and a struggling, second-year college student in those days found it difficult to come up with that payment. But I did it, and before long the little Belgium-made 20 with improved cylinder barrel was mine. I took my first and second deer with that gun. The open choke threw a slug just fine. Still would should I opt to use it. And had it not been the first gun I actually bought with my own funds, I likely would have traded it as well. But sentimentality got the better of me and I held on to it. Now a true classic, that little 20 would bring twice what I paid for it. But it is not for sale.

And in a stroke of good fortune, I stumbled into a gun shop some 20-plus years back. The proprietor plucked a real beauty from the rack and told me some guy had ordered it but failed to come up with the money. It was another A-5, this one a 12-gauge magnum with vent rib, Invector choke system, and the most striking stock and forearm wood I have ever seen on a production-line gun. While not built in Belgium as I wish it had been, it was still a Browning A-5. I wrote the gun-shop owner a check. A year or so later Browning announced that the A-5 was no more. A true classic had just become even more classical. Some new-fangled gas system was put into use to replace the recoiling system used in the A-5, and that signature Browning hump was going away. Tragic as I see it!

That 12, like its smaller 20-gauge cousin, has never failed. Since it is a big gun, I have used it only for turkeys and waterfowl, and this most judiciously. It still carries that grand luster it sported when new. And like the 20, it occupies a reverenced spot in the safe when not in use.

And when discussing classic shotguns, we must not overlook the doubles. These are an art form unto themselves, unlike anything else. And they should be side-by-sides in my way of thinking. There was a time when these were easily had, with several companies making solid working guns for the working individual. Not overly priced. Stevens doubles come to mind, and I had one of these. A 20 gauge choked modified and full. Those were the days before screw-in chokes. This double carried me through late high school and early college – before I got the A-5 20 previously mentioned. It went on many a squirrel, rabbit, quail, and duck hunt and always cast its load of lead exactly where I pointed it. If I missed I could never fault the gun. Oh, the Stevens was not as slick and refined as an L.C. Smith, but neither was it as expensive. It was just a solid gun that is now hard to find in good condition. How I very much long for that shotgun back in my hands. Or maybe it is that I simply long for those youthful days filled with abandon and poverty of worry. The Stevens was with me back then.

And there are classic rifles. That truly American invention, the Kentucky Long Rifle, stands at the forefront. This is a tool of elegance and grace. And it shoots as well as it looks. But for it to be a true classic, it must be an original or modern hand-built replication of the original. Factory-produced jobs won't compare. And you can pretty much omit an original. Too few remain in shootable condition, and those that do are too valuable to be taken afield. But get a skilled craftsman who understands the nuances of the Kentucky Rifle to build you one, and you have an immediate classic.

What about the lever rigs? Another collection of classics if taken from the late 19th and early 20th centuries. Winchester is king here, but others such as Marlin certainly hold their own. The Winchester that binds me most completely in its spell is the Model 92. Introduced in 1892, it was a dream come true for those who cherished smooth-running lever guns. Chambered in four calibers – .44-40, .38-40, .32-20, .25-20 – it was the epitome of the farm and ranch gun. It was the one in a saddle scabbard, the one behind the wagon seat, the one taken to the barn, the one that bounced around in those earliest of trucks, now classics themselves. It was perfect.

My number one squirrel rifle is none other than a Model 92. This particular rifle was built in 1895, the year that the .25-20 chambering was introduced. And that is its chambering – .25-20. Bruised and battered from years of use, it is still as smooth as ripple-free lake water at sundown. And a little .25-caliber lead bullet cast from a double-cavity mould and pushed by a diminutive charge of Unique powder will still stack in a ½-inch cluster at 30 yards. A perfect prescription for squirrels – and in a classic rifle at that!

There is another classic that I managed to acquire. This is the one Teddy Roosevelt called Big Medicine. This, too, was built by Winchester. It is the Model 1895, and its then-new box magazine permitted the use of pointed bullets. An original chambering was the .30-40 Krag. Roosevelt's son Kermit used this rifle/caliber extensively, and it was once considered the perfect combination for deer, black bears, elk, and moose. Teddy used the rifle in .405 Winchester, his favorite for lions, and this is the one he took to Africa. The Model 95 was later chambered in .30-06 as well.

Winchester occasionally makes a limited run of some of its old offerings. They did so in 2010 and a very few of the Model 95s hit the market. Calibers are, as you might guess, .30-40 Krag, .30-06 Springfield, and .405 Winchester. My order was miraculously filled for the 95 in .30-40!

And we certainly can't omit the single shots that are true classics. There are the Ballards and the Stevens. There is the Remington Rolling Block. There is the Winchester high wall and low wall. At least the Remington and Winchesters can still be had from the original companies in limited supply.

Then there is the one that is synonymous with single-shot rifles and familiar to practically anyone who knows anything about rifles and/or who has ever heard mention made of the great buffalo hunts on the Western plains in the 1870s. This one is the Sharps. A true Sharps, made from modern materials with the same design specifications as the first one from 1874 can be procured as a custom order from C. Sharps Rifle Company in Big Timber, Montana. Talk about a classic! Mine, chambered to the venerable old .45-70 introduced in 1873, has taken several whitetails. It will see its intended use recreated on the Kansas plains this upcoming October as it goes with me horseback in search of the wooly beast that fell to the Sharps in the late 19th Century. And it will, as its predecessors, shoot a charge of black powder and a 500-grain hand-cast lead bullet. My somewhat misplaced longing for the past will become reality.

We could go on and on with this discourse, but even then something would be left out that touches some reader somewhere. That was not intended. Not everything that can be considered a classic can be covered in one writing. But the fact remains that in the realm of firearms as well as art or machinery or literature, there are classics. They hold an appeal that the new can never replace. I feel extremely fortunate to have had and to have yet the opportunity to use some of the classic firearms. Perhaps the future will smile on me with even more such opportunity. That would be most welcome, for I dearly love classic firearms!

Kansas Whitetails:
Life's Good and Bad

Things were not looking good. Oh, the drive out to Kansas had been pleasant and relaxing for the most part. There was no rush, so Sam and I took our time. We stopped when we wanted, admired the countryside and talked about life's twists and turns with great abandon and reflection. Sam is a long-time friend and understands my circumstances as caregiver for parents. He was along to keep me company and had no plans to hunt. I was glad to have him.

I set my hunt up through Lee Hawes. Lee is a gentle sort who has hunted worldwide and has over the years, along with son Cody, put together a bison operation that is purely 1870s. I was fortunate to hunt those shaggy giants with him in the fall of 2010; that hunt now rates at the top of my outdoor experiences. While there in October 2010, we talked whitetails. I didn't feel that I needed a great deal of assistance if I could arrange a hunt, just a look at property boundaries. Lee obliged my request and agreed to be available via phone while he went about his trap line chores. And now, a year and two months after the bison hunt and much planning, I was in Kansas. Rifle season opened the next morning. Then one of those calamities of life.

Even before we got to the trailers that would serve as camp housing, my phone rang. Major difficulties at home. A bad diagnosis for my dad, a severe fall for my mom. I was needed there as quickly as possible. Additionally, that Kansas weather was in the process of change, and not for the better. Cold, wind, snow – all coming by the second day of season and predicted to stay for several more days. A sit-down with Lee was brought into play, along with several phone calls back home, and the decision was to rest that night, hunt the next day and then head back home the following. All were in agreement and things appeared under control, so this dramatically modified and less-than-perfect plan was set into motion. Far from ideal and much less than year-long hopes had envisioned, but necessary.

That evening we did some looking at properties to which I had access. A box blind had been set on a ridge near agricultural crops. A tiny stream bottom with cottonwoods was not far away. I would hunt there. The blind afforded a reliable view and would help thwart bitter winds that had already begun to batter those lonely hills. Before we got back to camp a grand buck appeared; he was ghosting a fence line on a neighboring property. Even in the growing twilight we made a reasonable assessment of his rack and put him in the 170 class. Maybe the following day – my only day to hunt – would be fruitful.

That day broke cold with 25- to 35-mph winds from the north. Clouds scudded overhead. Even within the confines of the box blind, a Cabela's Stand Hunter Extreme coat and heavy wool pants were needed to hold the chill at bay. But Sam and I were secure and carefully scanning the surrounding area with binoculars as daylight won its battle with a stubborn, frigid darkness.

My rifle was a Browning A-Bolt acquired the first year the A-Bolt became available. Chambered to .280 Remington and topped with a Leupold Vari-X III 3.5 – 10X scope, this rifle has served me well. Although I had a superb handload worked up for the .280, I opted for Hornady's Superformance 139 gr. SST factory fodder. Bench tests revealed this load to be as accurate as anything I had ever tried. It proved perfect before the day ended.

By midmorning a few deer had been spotted moving from fields to the cottonwoods. One was a huge-bodied specimen that we saw coming from the distance. He loped along as we marveled at his size and deep chest. But as he got closer we discovered that both sides of his rack had been broken off just above wrist-size bases. A victim of the rut that had not long passed. Not a candidate for the A-Bolt.

As the afternoon aged, a deer showed over near the cottonwoods. A buck. He trotted back and forth along the woods line and then turned in our direction. It was apparent that this was not a Kansas monster, but he was a good buck. Not unlike his comrade of earlier in the day, this one had a broken tine – the G2 on the right side. I determined years ago that all whitetails are magnificent, that all deserve full respect. So does any animal we hunt. Without hesitation I placed the crosshairs behind his shoulder and gently pressed the Browning's trigger. The SST worked its magic. My Kansas buck was down; the day was fading.

Tomorrow I would begin the drive home and face those arduous tasks that awaited. But today I gave thanks for the break I had been afforded and for the grand gift of nature and a whitetail buck I had been given.

That In-Between Time

Depending upon geography, many hunters find themselves in a familiar condition that occurs annually, that in-between time. And while this may not apply to areas such as Africa or New Zealand, it is definitely a quandary for those in the U.S. and Canada. There seems very little to do regarding hunting in summer, at least for a couple more months yet. But that is not totally accurate. There are a great many things to do. Perhaps these are not as exciting as hearing a bull elk bugle or waiting for a whitetail to tip along a trail, but available pursuits are adequately rewarding.

Obvious pastimes are building a new bow or a dozen arrows, but since these are indeed obvious, they will receive no additional comment here. Let's move to other elements that make up a hunter's year.

One, and again this depends a great deal on geography, is the establishment and/or maintenance of food plots. It could possibly be too late to do this in some regions, but in others the time is perfect. If it is a new plot you are dealing with, locating the site and making it ready for planting is something that will occupy your time and generate dividends come fall.

Select a plot site near cover. And if possible, set it up so that the approach route leaves that cover undisturbed. It may be necessary to open a trail to the plot to accomplish this, and that can be done and should be done during the off season, which is now. And keep prevailing winds in mind when selecting both the site and route. Even if you get to a plot silently, wind carrying scent into cover can spoil the situation.

Once a site is determined, clearing may need to be done. If so, brush from that clearing chore can be stacked in piles along the edges to enhance the plot's attractiveness. If legal and safe, burning is a viable tactic, and this can be employed when preparing a new plot or maintaining an existing plot.

Existing plots: Consider several things, among these mowing, fertilizer or lime application, disking, burning. Any one or a combination of these could be a positive in that plot's productivity. Assistance regarding such practices is generally available from sources such as a local County Agent, a farmer's cooperative, Natural Resources office or private consultants. There is no need to operate blindly in matters concerning food plots.

And there are other things that can be done during this in-between time. Try a little early scouting. Bucks and bulls will be deep into antler growth, and now is a good time to get out and see what is on the property you will hunt in September or October. Additionally, scouting now helps eliminate the possibility of spooking game too close to the actual hunt time. True, patterns will likely change with fall food sources, but early scouting can still be of great benefit. And if agricultural crops are in the area, a logical assumption can be gained regarding what foods will be available at harvest time, this generally coinciding with early bow season.

Back to those bows and arrows you are building during the summer months; get them done and start shooting. Go to the back yard, the woods, the 3-D range – anywhere to safely fling arrows. Keep in mind that it won't be too long before the fall hunting seasons will be here, though it is hard to imagine at the moment. All those in-between time efforts will then be appreciated.

The Roads of Life

Two roads diverged in a yellow wood and sorry I could not travel both and be one traveler; long I stood and looked down one as far as I could to where it bent in the undergrowth.

–Robert Frost

Those famous words by poet Robert Frost from "The Road Not Taken" are likely indicative of everyone, for if we are honest with ourselves and others, we have each stood looking toward the future and wondering which direction to take. This way or that way? Which of the two is the wiser route? Or does it truly matter which is selected as long as I (we) make prudent steps while on that course? There are likely more questions than answers.

Perhaps the most celebrated and cherished holiday seasons in American history are Thanksgiving and Christmas. These two are not only times of merriment but are times of reflection, each possessing deep meaning that stirs the very core of most. We openly recognize the gifts of life and the Gift of Christmas. While I was contemplating that celebration recently, Frost's words began to run through my mind.

Somewhat blinded when I came to that spot years ago where two roads diverged, I stood long – agonizing, wondering. I wanted to travel both, but as Frost concluded in his poem, that was not the option. Select one and begin the journey. That I did. Some steps along the way proved treacherous – rocky, rugged, not easily negotiated. But the only way to a destination is to stay the route that leads there. And the journey itself is to be embraced, even the hills and rocky outcroppings. For it is the journey that is greater than the destination.

One line of Frost's poem states: *I shall be telling this with a sigh somewhere ages and ages hence.* Those ages and ages have, to some degree, come in my life. As a result, I can now more accurately tell this story, some portions of it with a sigh and some with joyous abandon. Such is life.

The road I determined less traveled has led to fulfillment. There have been three professions, all somewhat similar but different enough to be dissimilar. Each has been filled with satisfaction, rewards. Each has granted deep friendships and extraordinary experiences. There were tears and laughter. There was sadness and joy. There is now contentment.

The road I chose has provided loving family members, both blood kin and extended, who share the same values as I. It has afforded the opportunity to speak, in various forms, to thousands of individuals, to be a part of their lives if only in words taken from a page somewhere. It has, even in the hazardous climb of its ragged peaks, permitted support from those who cared and wished me safely over the cliffs and into peaceful valleys. It has given in multiples rare glimpses of God's creation seen by few. And in this holiday season I must reflect upon the fact that the road chosen has granted me a more thorough understanding of Thanksgiving and the Christmas Gift.

Frost closed his poem with these words: *Two roads diverged, and I…I took the one less traveled by. And that has made all the difference.*

Indeed!

And Finally, Spring!

Could be just my perception of the situation, but it seems this past winter was particularly pronounced. Barren and bleak at times, decorated in a breathtaking white at others, it maintained its grandeur, its peculiar spell that binds and promotes reflection. But it was clearly winter, unlike many we experience here in the Deep South.

And toward its conclusion I found myself laid up with back surgery. Just a simple procedure that required an entry through the throat to get to a troublesome ruptured disc that necessitated the fusion of two vertebras. An enjoyable process for anyone who prefers pain! But even in all that, hope emerged. This first evidenced itself during a requisite short walk down the driveway and around the edge of the pasture in front of my house.

With cane and neck brace, I eased along and soaked up sunshine on a blustery morning. And there, just over a bit from my route and under a collection of oaks, were the robins. Five or six of them skittered about with great abandon, their curious chirps rippling across the brisk air not yet warmed by spring. But their presence promised that season's coming.

And there were a couple of squirrels. Not unlike the robins, they scooted about in the fresh air. One bounced away, stationed himself at the base of a tree and gave me a thorough scolding. I forgot the temporary discomfort and smiled. On a feeder just outside the window was a collection of chickadees, their tiny, subdued chatter a welcome addition to the day. A goldfinch interrupted their reverie.

Crows were also busy that morning. They cawed and fussed and darted about in the sky overhead as jays stiff-legged along and called one to the other. Somewhere, out there hidden in the branches, a mockingbird sang. It suddenly became apparent that change was in the making. Winter was losing its hold in favor of more temperate conditions. Life was moving as it always does and should. Not stagnant as it at first might appear.

Then an epiphany! Life is cyclical. Spring breaks the chains of winter and everything refreshes. Dross is burned away with sunshine and newness. Scars heal. The cold relinquishes its grip. Living is once again an exercise that we could barely imagine only days earlier. All this is visible in nature.

By now that distant spring is reality. Blooms and blossoms protrude from various plants. That withered and browned grass is putting on its chlorophyll makeup. The oaks and hickories have sent out new hands that reflect a glorious glow as they applaud and dance in an April breeze.

In a woodlot somewhere a wild turkey struts and gobbles, his head and waddles showing red and white and blue. He postures to his comrades, wings dragging and fan flared. He is almost grotesque in his grandness.

And a bluegill smacks a morsel from the water's surface. That quiet, quaint kiss is the epitome of wildness. It shouldn't be missed. In areas to the north, a rainbow trout scoots from beneath a rock in a fast-flowing stream to scoop up some diminutive insect, his iridescence a gaudy and impressive spectacle. A largemouth moves about the shallows near emerging lily pads or within a submerged stump field.

The whitetail buck has lost his antlers, but sooner than it

seems reasonable these will begin to grow again and adorn him with that crown that is his identity come fall. The does are heavy with fawn. Thumbnail-sized eggs crack so that equally small bird chicks can enter the world. There will be a great deal of flitting back and forth to and from the nests by the adults who tote worms and bugs to the young.

And somewhere along the way, perhaps next month or the next, life will slow with the approach of summer. The deer will seek out shade. The turkeys will ghost silently through the woods. The birds will concentrate much of their activity to early mornings and late afternoons. The leaves will drip with early dew and rattle with warm rains. This is just another one of those changes that are pertinent to life in nature.

But for now, it is finally spring. And it is a glorious time to be alive.

September's Songs

Attempting to visualize a pleasant September day while in the midst of an August heat wave is an arduous task. But the recall of such days is strong enough to speak for itself and provide a vivid picture if presented with sufficient accuracy. That is certainly the intent here, for September possesses a peculiar hold on my memory, on my entire being. It is a month of pure magic.

Perhaps the allure of September creeps in on the breeze of promised change. It is subtle and quiet in its entry, but it does arrive with adequate authority to assure the observant that summer is somewhere behind and autumn is around the next bend. The month is a time of transition.

While there are a great many things appealing about September, it is the music it provides that most impacts me. Songs if you will. Orchestrated and performed not by humanity but by nature and its Creator. Often difficult to hear, or at least a proper venue for hearing is often difficult to find, these songs fill the air and allow the spirit to soar. From melancholy to euphoric, this music moves the one it reaches.

Perhaps a favorite among September's songs is the call of a pileated woodpecker. The tune is not restricted to this month alone, but it is definitely available in abundance to the careful listener. Haunting and distant and mysterious, the cry can be unnerving to one unfamiliar with it. But coming to know it and grasping its wildness soothes any tremors of alarm and replaces them with a sense of reverence and well-being scarcely found otherwise.

I recall with great clarity my first hearing of this marvelous song. It was in the Pearl River swamp with my dad, and we were hunting squirrels for supper. He was the hunter; I was the tag-along boy eager to learn and experience something that would shape my entire life. The resonance came from across woods near Collier House Lake, a non-descript slough long abandoned by the river. I shuddered. "Indian hen," he said. Then I saw the bird, darting in that up-and-down flight common to the species. From that day until now, that clarion of the pileated woodpecker fills me with wanderlust and the warmth of all-rightness.

And there is another musical offering, this one a veritable symphony. It is less prominent than that of the woodpecker, but it is equally impressive, enchanting. Part of the difficulty in hearing this is its preference for specific concert halls. Just any stage will not do; it demands attention to detail. The best place I have found is beside a sun-parched but still-standing corn field in some quiet bottom with woods and hills and grass patches, perhaps even a ditch nearby. Once such a probable spot is found, it is incumbent upon the visitor to remove any other sources of noise and concentrate fully upon the surroundings. It is then and there that the symphony will begin – a melody not unlike Brahms, a grand lullaby.

Listen! Over there is the cricket. And out that way is the drone of the katydid. The hum of the grasshopper is added for variety. Maybe even a jay proffers an eighth note to the chord. And if all is perfect, there will be enough wind to rattle those tattered and twisted corn stalks as percussion. Not much is required; just a tiny wisp that can notify the cheeks and nose that there is indeed a moving of air will do it. And the combined sounds are grandiose. One could fall into a quiet nap while sitting beneath an oak or beside a fence post in the presence of such music.

Want more? Go to a stream. Most such waters will be low and gentle. But somewhere, not far upstream or down, is a log jam or clay bottom or some other structure around which the water flows. There will be music. A gurgle or a splash. It will serenade. And it, like all the others, will be magical. One of September's songs.

A Winter Walk

Some may contend that winter in Mississippi is impover-
ished when beauty is sought. True, unless we have snow to smooth
out the rough edges and highlight the hillsides, surroundings can be
a bit austere. But that blanket of white is a veritable stranger, and
waiting for it is a waste of productive time.

I must disagree with those who see winter as completely
bleak. There is a strange sort of grandeur available if one goes in
search of it, and a typical woodlot is the perfect place to find it.
Majesty is scattered all about, and now is the time to experience
that offering.

So what will you see on a winter walk in the woods? That
depends on a great many things: location, duration, time of day,
stealth. You will certainly see hardwoods virtually stripped of leaves.
These fell earlier and are now crunching under foot and becoming a
part of the soil. Beeches will yet have leaves, these browned and
curled and withered by winter's cold, and they present an odd contrast to the skeletal forms afforded by the oaks and hickories and
sweet gums. Green? A scattering here and there: pine, cedar, holly,
some vine plants. But most of the surroundings are naked. That,
however, does not mean there is no life, no things of beauty.

I have always been of the opinion that a bare oak, its

branches reaching into an azure sky, is a thing of great enchantment. Haunting. This persuasion likely goes back to childhood,
when I first began to notice such things and associate them with
life on that small farm; the association remains. Those oaks are a re-
minder, a sentinel that gives notice to the cycles of nature. And if
nothing else, they indicate that life renews, that spring will come
again.

There may be no sight more reflective and endearing than a
winter sunrise seen through undressed hardwoods. Shafts of light
begin to filter to the forest floor, creating tiny sparkles on frosted
ground. Mist drifts upward as rays push away the chill. The day
awakes, and with it come all forms of life.

If turkeys are present, they begin their conversation. First a
few soft clucks and yelps, and then a chorus erupts as the big birds
prepare for a day of foraging. Cackles and heavy wing beats announce that the turkeys have left their roost and are now on the
ground.

Whitetails begin to ghost back into cover. Maybe a big-
eyed doe will creep by. Perhaps a buck is yet following her in these
final days of the rut. His antlers are still in place, but will soon fall
to the ground and become food for rodents. And that buck's scrapes
will be visible for several weeks, these markings trailed along ridges,
woods roads, and field edges.

Crows will caw. Pileated woodpeckers will flit from tree to
tree, their raucous calls echoing across the mystery of morning.
Chickadees will chatter. Water droplets on frosty limbs will glisten
as the sun gains purchase in the sky and will pitter-patter downward with the warmth.

Squirrels will become active. They will bounce from one
limb to another and scurry down tree trunks to busy themselves
with buried acorns. Their nests are never so visible as now. These are
those big leafy clusters that seem to hang precariously in the high
forks. Just yesterday I saw a fat gray squirrel scoot into its nest in a

big oak as I approached. I was not a threat, but the squirrel seemed in no mood to take chances. I smiled.

If your winter walk encompasses midday, there will likely be a breeze. It will rustle those few leaves clinging to the trees and produce peaceful music akin to the finest symphony. And if you can remain until sunset, that time will be as glorious as the early morning. The woods will darken and the shadows lengthen. Most wildlife will quicken for a brief time and then slow to stillness as the cold begins to win its struggle for dominance. The sun will drop low and then disappear, leaving only the tentacles of winter in silhouette.

But if you want to take a winter walk and see its true essence, do it now. In little more than a month that same ambience will not be present. It will be morphing; it will be decorated with the hint of spring. A winter walk will then have to wait another year.

The River of Reflections

January: This river is placid. No roiling rapids or thunderous whitewater here. And save the distant chatter of a pileated woodpecker and gentle rustle of a winter wind through naked willows, all is quiet. Quiet is good, for there is far too little of it to go around this day and time.

I sit beside an old slough and look for wood ducks. I want wood duck breast dredged in milk and flour, lightly salted and peppered and fried over medium heat for supper. The little outboard that pushed a small boat upstream to this locale disturbed an abundance of these ducks as I made progress toward the destination. They broke water in every twist and turn and from practically every tangle along the way.

I look around at this old slough, a familiar locale that dates back to childhood. It was on that bluff just over there that I took my first squirrel. It was in this very slough that I caught my first bluegill, both happenings under the patient guidance of my dad. And it was over there a way that we country-neighbor boys built a ragged cabin on July 4th in the mid 1960s. High school days. And it did afford us a form of independence, fitting to the day of its construction. We camped in it every Friday night for two years with no interruptions in the schedule. Life eventually scattered us and broke up the camping regimen, but the memories are as real and poignant as ever. I reflect.

It was in this area that we chased rabbits with great abandon – big, long-running swamp rabbits that taxed my pair of short-legged beagles at every opportunity. And if memory serves correctly, it was just down the woods road there that I saw my first deer. He was a huge old buck that Herman and Homer disturbed one morning from an oak flat as they tried to sort out a rabbit's path. Two of us were there that day, and we stood in opened-mouth amazement as this buck bounded away from the ruckus.

I hear wings zipping through the winter sky. A wood duck drake and two hens sail past and circle. My old A-5 comes to shoulder in anticipation of their return, and seconds later they commit to the slough. The drake drops from the trio at the shotgun's blast and splashes down, a spectacular creature even in this termination. His colors are brilliant. That same wind that has reddened my cheeks and numbed my fingers pushes him to the edge where I can reach him with a stick. I admire this incredible, gaudy specimen and feel that familiar twinge of sorrow. The hunt is over. One duck is all I need. But I seize this opportunity to sit and think.

This river is an integral part of my life. Has always been. My grandfather and dad once owned the property that skirts the stream, so I had full access to it during my growing-up years. Access is now limited, but that river still touches my spirit. It seems to flow through my veins. There was a time when I thought I owned it, but I have come to see that I never did and never could. I have grown to realize that the more accurate conclusion is the river owns me. I cannot separate myself from it. And that is as it should be. The river will be here long after I have passed from the scene, and it will continue to touch, to influence lives.

Before I leave a sobering thought enters my mind. I came in search of wood ducks, but I found myself. And since this river has so impacted my life from the earliest years on into these latter ones, should it not also play a part in the end? Perhaps a resting place on that bluff would be in order, or the scattering of ashes in the turbid current would be fitting. Seems only natural. For this river, this river of reflections, runs throughout my being.

Enamored of Tents

I can't recall when I first became enamored of tents. That fascination goes back to childhood when I would fashion rough shelters from a cotton sheet or tattered quilt or remnant of a canvas tarp once used to cover a pickup load of cotton. I even set up a rather attractive wedge configuration with some sweetgum poles and worn blanket, the latter from a World War II surplus store. I was most pleased and somewhat amazed at how that structure turned the summer rains in those days of innocence.

I got my first real tent when I was 12 years old. It was a green canvas thing that was basically a cone. It had a semi "V" flap that could be pulled out and set with poles to form an awning and dropped down at night to secure two or three country boys from the elements. And those poles, like the ones used with the blanket, were sweetgum cut from fence rows behind the house.

That tent was a grand acquisition. It took us well into the teenage years and would likely be with me today had it not been for one of my dad's bull yearlings. He managed to creep into the tent through an untied side of the flap to investigate this strange thing that was perched beneath a tree in his pasture home. Upon our noisy return at dusk to our camp, the yearling thought better of his initial decision to enter and exited with great gusto, this time in a location where there was no flap. Poles snapped and the tent exploded. Camp was closed!

Then came three small wedges, all canvas and all purchased from an Army surplus store. Six of us bought them in community fashion, and that is the way they were used – as a community. All set like the fingers of a star with their fronts to the fire. It was a glorious scene, one repeated with tremendous regularity for several years.

After these wedge tents came a big one, a 10 x 16. Again a community effort by several boys whose only income was earned picking cotton or cleaning out chicken houses. That one, if such a thing were possible, saw more use than the three smaller units. We camped. Grand times, all.

And then came what most would consider the more modern tents. And they were. They were made of nylon and had a rain fly. The space between the tent and fly allowed for more ventilation and helped eliminate that muggy, sticky feeling common to canvas in hot weather. They, too, served well. I still have two among my collection.

I suppose, however, that if I were forced to choose my favorite tent for all endeavors, it would have to be the canvas wall tent. This proclivity no doubt found its genesis in my early reading of outdoor magazines and the exploits of those fortunates who found themselves camped in such a tent somewhere in the wilds of Colorado or Idaho or Africa, a pipe out the tent's roof puffing smoke from a wood-stove fire. How could life be better? I wondered as I clambered through those pages in sheer delight. As it turns out, life can't be better. I speak those words now from experience. Wanderlust led me to visit such places, to make a canvas wall tent my place of abode, to stoke the stove and ward off the chill. I even weathered a three-day blizzard in Montana's Missouri Breaks in such a tent when the thermometer dropped to an honest 21 degrees below zero.

So what makes a tent so alluring? It is the smell of treated canvas. It is the sound of raindrops on the fly. It is the chirp of insects, separated from you but only inches away. It is the crackle of the campfire just outside the flap. It is the feel of soft grass or pine straw beneath the bedroll. It is the cry of the owl or the whippoorwill or the coyote or the wolf in the distance. It is the rush of a mountain stream that lulls you to sleep. It is the clarion of sunrise that comes in the form of the cardinal's brisk chattering or the crow's raucous cawing or the squirrel's boisterous scolding or the turkey's lusty gobbling. All are perfectly and intimately absorbed from a tent.

Love Affair With Rural Living

While this statement may sound perilously close to lyrics from some country song, it is absolute truth: I was born country! Plowing-a-gray-mule-in-a-cotton-patch country. In fact, the mule's name was Grady. Growing-a-garden-and-feeding-the-chickens-and-milking-the-cow country. And there was that troublesome chore of butchering hogs for sausage and bacon and ham and pork chops. All these were an integral part of that life I have come to love more now as an aging adult than I did as a child.

I have not always lived in the country. Like many, I moved away for college and later moved even farther away to attend graduate school. A master's degree plus some additional studies behind me, I fell into a work regimen in various venues, this work associated with cities such as New Orleans. Subdivision living had its pleasantries, and I adapted fairly well to rush-hour traffic. Even came to the conclusion that I would always live in this fashion and removed from my country roots. But that tie, that bonding, would never let me rest. Then one day a frightening but hopeful decision was made. I came home – to the country.

Some may ask, "Why, with all the convenience and modern attraction of the cities, would anyone want to live in the country, to digress if you will?" Any answer will carry with it a great many variables, and each individual will have his or her response. I can address such thinking only from my perspective.

Country is home for me. My roots run deeply into the sod of the area in which I now live. That is perhaps the overriding factor in it all. But there are other reasons, some of which may or may not appeal to anyone else.

I enjoy the space, that open quality common to the country. And I like the uniqueness of each homestead. Similar to others around it to a degree, but different in its ambience, revealing the proclivity of its owner. There may be a new brick house with huge columns and hard-surface circle drive here, and just around the curve an old but well-kept frame structure, azaleas and magnolias adorning its yard, some child's grandparents puttering about with a hoe or rake. A vegetable garden will be out back. A dog will be asleep on the porch or under the shrubs.

And everyone around knows that dog, knows the dogs of other neighbors as well. These dogs are generally welcome wherever they roam, and they are likely to get a pat on the head at every stop along their travels. "Molly came to visit me the other day," someone will say. "She is a sweet dog." Or, "Your old dog, Lady, came around to the shed and spoke when I stopped by there to pick up that spreader. I told her you said it was okay, and she went back to her nap."

I enjoy early mornings in the country, dew dripping from trees and the world fully alive, absent the noise of cities. A squirrel jumps from one limb to the next, sending a shower of droplets to the ground. In the distance a tractor drones its lonesome melody, while birds of all description perform a symphony, percussion provided by a woodpecker on a tall snag. And in spring, if I am fortunate, a turkey adds his gobble to the music, something akin to the cannon blast in the "1812 Overture."

And just outside the back door some 30 yards, where I stop mowing, there are blackberries. They shimmer in the morning sun. Homemade jelly from their earlier siblings rests peacefully in the pantry, waiting for hot biscuits and a winter breakfast. All these things are part of the country I know and love.

Do I ever consider moving? From time to time, yes. But even that centers around some pastoral setting. I am home – in the country. My next major move from here will be facilitated by the local undertaker.

A Dream in Kansas

In my dream, that plaintive cry of coyotes drifted across short-grass prairie, riding a cold wind that shuffled about in sparse vegetation and chilled all it touched. That same wind made protracted jabs at the smoke flaps of the tipi and fluttered the canvas before heading over a landscape of dry washes and rolling hillsides on to Mulberry Creek and points beyond. I, in this state of disturbed sleep, retreated progressively deeper into my sleeping bag, an instinctive reaction to this surreal setting.

And then a horse nickered. Close. The rustle of corn being poured into a feed bucket had prompted the vocalization, and I startled to full alert. This was no dream. This was reality. Those cries of the coyotes and the short-grass prairie and the ubiquitous wind and the tipi and the horses were real. Just out there, on the other side of a canvas wall, was the world of 1874. I was indeed in Kansas, and for the next three days I would hunt bison in a setting that has not changed since those magnificent and historic shaggy beasts flowed by the millions in undulating waves across this haunting real estate.

The American bison, commonly called buffalo, is the key player in a drama of tragedy and triumph. These animals were the staple of life for thousands of Native Americans scattered about from South Texas northward. These various tribes relied on the buffalo for food, shelter, and clothing, but the westward movement of settlers from the eastern regions would soon prove a disaster, both for the natives and the bison. A strong demand for the hides of these monstrous beasts created an opportunity for market hunters, and these pretty much wiped the bison off the Earth.

But not quite. A few were saved. And they were saved by an unlikely party – a buffalo hunter, Jessie "Buffalo" Jones of Garden City, Kansas. Jones captured a small collection of calves, and from that and similar efforts the bison returned. They are now well established throughout a great part of their original range. Such is the case on property owned by Lee Hawes of Ford, Kansas.

When I learned of Lee's operation, I was sure this was the place I wanted to go and hunt bison. Hawes allows some limited hunting each year to keep the herd on his property in balance with the habitat, and this he does in the same manner as it was done in 1874 – horseback, tipi and dugout camps, black-powder cartridge rifles, and no modern conveniences. Just the prairie camp and the bison. He even encourages dressing in 1870s fashion. And Lee's ranch, which was settled by his great-grandfather Judge Hawes who drove cattle from Texas and became a friend with Bat Masterson when Masterson was the law of Dodge City, was never plowed and converted to farming or non-native grasses suitable for cattle. It remains as it was and is now an island in the middle of modern agriculture.

I awoke that first morning, as described above, to a world completely unlike the one I left behind. Armed with a .45-70 C. Sharps Bridgeport "buffalo" rifle still built today in Big Timber, Montana, and a collection of hand-cast lead bullets loaded with Goex FFg black powder, I stepped outside to experience something I had only imagined. The load development and shooting practice had consumed the past few months, and now I was actually there where the wind whips the grasses and the buffalo roam about with abandon as they did in the 19th Century and before.

It was late afternoon of the second day before I was able to sort out the bull I would take from the herd. There were perhaps 200 of them on a pan-flat area with no cover through which to crawl for concealment, so guide Cody Hawes suggested we dismount, turn my horse loose so that he would graze or go back to camp, and then walk beside his horse in a diagonal approach toward the herd. It worked, and approximately one-half hour after getting settled on the shooting sticks and releasing Cody's horse to do the same as mine had done, the bull of choice presented a shot. There was the thunderous rumble of a heavy black-powder charge, the blue-gray smoked drifting away on that ever-present wind. The bull was down.

As afternoon light faded, I knelt beside an incredible creature whose ancestors provided sustenance for generations of Native Americans. The wind stirred through his thick, handsome mane. I thought of the great tragedy associated with the bison and the very real success in returning these animals to the areas where they belong. I stroked that mane and admired the perfection of an animal built for the extremes in which he lived. Tears filled my eyes, an appropriate response to such an event, and I removed my hat, bowed my head and gave thanks. A dream had become reality.

Nature's Beauty Abundant in Winter's Austerity

Winter dominates. Few are those pleasant days that beckon one to venture into wild places away from warmth and shelter. Gone are those spectacular color shows of autumn. Spring blossoms are yet too distant to quicken hopes for change. Some might argue that there is nothing to see apart from obvious austerity.

And there is some truth in that. Save the odd beech or oak that has clung tenaciously to its foliage, leaves are gone. Even those remaining are brown and curled. But beauty remains. It comes more in the form of light and shadow than it previously did in color. Properly set on the horizon at sunrise or sunset, even those naked arms and fingers of big timber afford an alluring portrait, haunting though it may be. It all comes down to what the observer looks for and sees.

Consider an early-morning field or woods edge or lawn covered with frost. It dances and sparkles and is filled with motion, with life of a different sort not available at any other time. As sunlight pushes misty tentacles through bare branches and kisses the ground, a gradual unfolding of majesty occurs. The frost at first reflects that light in twinkling diamonds that stir the senses. This may prompt an unexpected exhaling of excited breath, which rises toward heaven in a gleeful fog. Then the frost is slowly transformed. It gives off a smoky salute and vanishes in a sigh of warmth. Short lived, to be sure, but simply too marvelous to miss.

Look, also, to a late afternoon. Day ends in a grand display of orange red. These settings, if listened to carefully, speak. Their proclamation can be sober, painting the passing of time. But they can also be comforting, a time for reflection. And like their opposites of 10 hours earlier, they are too good, too important to miss.

So, if the austerity of winter becomes overpowering and drives you to a search for beauty, bundle up and go outside. Listen intently. Watch judiciously. Beauty is at the core of even a winter's day.

Dog Graveyard:
Paying Respect to Good Friends

Barney is the only dog buried here that I knew well. She got her unlikely masculine name because the Carruth family found her abandoned at their barn. And not unlike her name, what she became was unlikely as well. Barney developed into the finest flush dog I have ever seen. She would sit patiently on the wagon, trembling with anticipation as high-strung pointers sorted out the quail. Upon command Barney was off like a bolt of lightning, putting up a covey or singles that rocketed from the well-manicured bird cover at Millbrook Plantation. And when some hunter connected, Barney was the first to rush in for a retrieve, proudly toting a quail in her whiskered jaws and gingerly delivering it to her owner, Dr. Ed Carruth. Her passing was sad.

"Barney's burial was the most upsetting to me," says Dr. Carruth. "I think I cried three days. I still shed a tear when I stop by her grave." That, in my opinion, speaks well of the man. Doc acquired Millbrook Plantation at Stonewall, Mississippi, many years ago and has transformed it into a quail hunter's delight. He has dedicated aproximately 800 acres to enhanced quail habitat, and the setting is ideal. His staff, consisting of Randy Freeman, Hunt Master/Farm Manager; Stanley Herrington, Head Guide; John Kennon and Greg Chandler, guides; Carol Bateman, cook; Myra Southern, housekeeping; and Sammy Donald, who does chores and is responsible for cleaning quail, all take their jobs seriously and provide exceptional service to quail hunters.

"The Dog Graveyard idea started with Tip, my first German Wirehair (Drathaar) who died I think about 1999," Carruth recalls. "He was my introduction to the breed and was a top bird dog. But in addition to that, he was my pet and my friend, too good a dog to be buried just anywhere. So I picked that spot on a well-drained piney hill overlooking a favorite quail plot and the pond he loved to swim. He deserved and received a marker and short epitaph: Tip – Friend and Companion. After that, it was only natural to bury our dogs next to Tip. And for all I tried to create a short epitaph fitting to each individual dog."

Carruth reflects once more on Barney. "She is the only one who got a custom-made pine casket with velvet lining. Her epitaph is exactly what I always told her she was: The Best Dog in the Whole Wide World. I think she would actually smile when I told her that.

"The next most tearful for me [after Barney] was Gussie, a Drathaar. She was also a combination working dog and pet and stayed in the house with us. The Drathaars make good companions and pets and can still be top hunting dogs.

"And burying Kellis, my big ole chocolate lab, who flushed and retrieved for us, was also pretty painful. Her epitaph is simple: She Was a Good Ole Dog. She spent a lot of time riding with me in my truck. Kellis lived to be 14."

Grave markers and epitaphs are many, and as years pass these will surely grow. But that is all a part of living. Loss is a given. It is never easy or minus pain, but the joy that comes before the sorrow is worth the hurt. Pleasant recall grows richer and more intense as the ache gradually subsides.

And there can be no better way to honor and remember these special animals that lived for quail hunting than to make their final resting place a secluded hillside overlooking the habitat that felt their foot falls and reverberated with their enthusiasm. The Dog Graveyard at Millbrook is well done.

Autumn's Magic
Through the Hunter's Eyes

Mystique is a fitting word when describing autumn. The season is filled with it. Appealing yet haunting, refreshing yet sobering, a beginning yet an end – autumn exhibits a broad spectrum of sentiments. And the most vivid, lucid portrait of this season is often seen through the hunter's eyes.

Part of autumn's appeal to the hunter is nothing more than simple anticipation. But anticipation plays a significant role in life, whether we are hunters or not. Looking forward to some event gives strength to move in that direction. We often need such impetus, for strength can be depleted in the mundaneness of the everyday. Anticipation coaxes, encourages, calls us to act. It is a rudimentary ingredient in the prescription that prevents stagnation.

For the hunter that anticipation may focus on a chilly morning in the squirrel woods, senses quickened and attuned to the slightest rustle of a shaking limb. Or it may be that associated with the rhythmic crunch of leaves as a whitetail approaches the stand. Or that faint whistle of wings at tree-top height as sunrise brushes back the darkness along a river slough. Whatever the anticipator anticipates, it has a peculiar and life-bringing appeal.

And we must not overlook the pure glory when considering

autumn's appeal. A color show unmatched. An azure sky. A carefully orchestrated symphony of sights and sounds and smells.

Yet, it is all rather haunting. The ghost riding an autumn sunset. The breeze-induced quiver of withered leaves. The resultant shudder that runs up the spine of anyone who sees and hears and contemplates. The hunter, perhaps more than some, absorbs these elements. Alluring but haunting.

Autumn is refreshing. Gone is the oppression of summer's heat, this replaced by the brisk and the clean. The participant in autumn's renewal is prompted to wander and wonder and consider, to wear a ragged coat and felt hat. The hunter may do this alone or in the company of others, perhaps children or grandchildren or parents or grandparents. He or she is at liberty to reflect on the past and hope for the future in such company. He or she is at liberty to shed a tear for the losses of yesterday and posture a smile for the possibilities of tomorrow.

Yet, it is all rather sobering. Few times of the year bring on the reflective qualities in us all as does autumn, regardless of how deeply these qualities may be buried within our beings. We think of what was and what was not and what might have been. We think of what may come. We hunters interrupt our stalk for game to rummage through neglected tombstones we happen across or to touch a tiny track left by an equally tiny animal that was busy with life along a sand ditch or to watch a dead leaf let go from its place of prominence and drift to the forest floor to lie among the millions of others that will return to the earth which sustained the tree that gave them life. We are sobered by it all.

Autumn is a beginning. For the hunter, autumn is the beginning of the hunting seasons, a time offering untold opportunities to pursue game. This potential stirs the hunter's spirit. This stirring may not be so much the actual collection of that game as it is the hope and possibility of doing so, that anticipation mentioned above if you will. And it happens in autumn – the beginning.

Yet, it is also the end. In the greater scheme of things, this beginning amounts to a miniscule portion of the total, a short-lived occurrence in the day-to-day. In reality, the autumn beginning signals the year's end. Winter comes. However, spring is not far away. A new and spectacular rebirth waits. Not unlike life I must say.

The Retirement of an Old Friend

It has been said upon great authority that if a man comes to the end of his life and can claim even one individual as a true friend, that man is indeed blessed. There is merit in that statement. A true friend is far more than a simple acquaintance on some electronic gadget, is more revered than an occasional companion. That true friend is a cherished treasure that remains the same regardless of circumstances, one who can be counted on to see our faults and care just the same. Most difficult to find and nurture – true friendship.

So in the light of such an august and reverential description of a true friend, it seems ill placed to attach the word to some inanimate object. But in full recognition that no object can approach the status of human friendship and with sincere apologies for this upcoming precarious proclamation, I wish to announce that I retired from use an old friend recently. This friend was a basic broadhead built in some factory for the express purpose of riding the tip of a hunting arrow. Still, it possessed traits we seek in a living, breathing friend and that friend, carefully chosen and well developed, possesses traits I found in that broadhead.

The broadhead came in a package with five others some 30 years ago. Nondescript when I removed it from the cardboard container, it was very much the same as its counterparts. Only time would set it apart. I suppose I came to recognize it as a specific and separate entity when I took a deer with it. That day I recovered the arrow and tossed it in the back of my truck, that broadhead in perfect condition save its dulled edges.

At some point later, maybe five years, I came across that arrow/broadhead combo, the arrow warped and of no use. I inspected the broadhead. Due to my lack of attention earlier, there was some rust. I oiled and polished the head and then took a file to its edges. Perfectly serviceable, not unlike a true human friend we may have neglected. I removed it from the damaged arrow and put it on another aluminum shaft. Those were my days of weakness, when I had opted to shoot a compound bow. The very next month that same tip took another deer for my freezer.

I am happy to report that the madness of technology held me in its grip for only a season or two. I gladly, and with irrevocable resolve, went back to archery as I had known it and as it should be – recurves, longbows, primitive Osage staves, cedar arrow shafts. That rust-speckled head made the transition as well, and we were both back in our intended element. Any true friend will follow through those shadows of confusion and misdirection.

During ensuing years that same head, this time cast by a custom-build recurve, took a huge Mississippi hog that produced more pork than I thought possible. It later sailed from a bamboo-backed Osage longbow and claimed a Delta deer. It then went with me to Tennessee and put more pork in the freezer, all these excursions separated by a scattering of years. The most recent successful use of it came on a Texas ranch this past January while I was toting a newly built Osage take-down longbow that Mike Yancey and I had built in September before this hunt. Another hog. I particularly enjoy wild pork!

And just this past week, as this is written, the veteran broadhead joined me on that same Texas ranch for a much-anticipated turkey hunt. All seemed well. Turkeys gobbled; large flocks drifted by and talked incessantly with me as I mimicked the clucks and purrs and yelps they were executing. And then a single gobbler – puffed up and proud and curious. He came to a halt at 14 yards from my station. And while that may seem an incredibly short distance, it is more than far enough with a longbow and such a diminutive target deceitfully obscured by a proliferation of iridescent feathers. The draw was smooth, the release felt right, and the arrow was on its way. It went low.

After the proverbial dust settled, I left my hide and went to inspect the situation in an effort to determine if I heard and saw what I thought I heard and saw. I did. The arrow smacked solidly into a rock just beyond the gobbler and lay quietly there. No marks of a hit save to the rock. I thought all was well outside the miss, but upon closer inspection I learned that the head had suffered irreparable damage. The cedar shaft, pushing the tip with great force, had powdered its way into the ferrule and caused that ferrule to separate from the blade. The head's use as a hunting tool had ended.

Back here at home, I removed the broadhead from the shaft and gently laid it on a shelf in my office. It has lost its usefulness to a degree, but I will save it. For you see, like that true friend who slows with age and perhaps can no longer explore high and wild places, simply seeing that individual – or that broadhead – refreshes memory of past experiences shared. That is likely the most important element of friendship in the first place!

September Memories
and Outdoor Wonders

Attempts to live in the past are futile. The only viable options have been established: Progression or stagnation. Still, I can't resist those occasionally deep and often protracted journeys into reminiscence each year as September casts its mystical spell across the landscape and through my aging recall.

And not surprisingly, many of those journeys – if not all those journeys – in one way or another relate to the outdoors. Not exclusively to hunting or fishing, though these were and are certainly an integral part for me and likely anyone else with a similar mindset, but to the outdoors in general. For it was in these alfresco settings that my childhood was spent.

Squirrel season was the most heralded hunting event in these parts and in those days when I was young. And while it did not open in September, that month gave ample cause to begin thinking about and planning for those grandiose adventures that would come soon. The black gum leaves would turn brown and red then as they do now, and some few would rattle to the ground to rest silently on warm sand along wooded streams and ditches or among the long grasses bordering field-edge roads. These leaves were an epiphany, a proclamation of things to come. They always generated a swirl of enthusiasm. That has not changed.

At some point during all this, my dad and I would pull out battered single-barrel shotguns and rummage through tattered tan game vests. The latter held what we hoped was a sufficient supply of leftover shells: 20 gauge, No. 6 shot, high-brass paper hulls. The guns received a cursory squirt of 3-In-One machine oil. I can still smell that magic elixir, which remains a capable cure for most ailments. No trip to the Big Island or the Coast of Maine now could produce the degree of exhilaration which that pedestrian practice of gun cleaning did back then.

Even during those times of farm labor, some of it arduous, the lure of September managed to creep into the crevices of my being, those external crevices soiled and beaded with sweat-soaked dust and plant debris common to harvest. The internal crevices were far more antiseptic, but September reached and excited them as well. The rustle of dried and curled corn stalks giving up their chubby ears of yellow sustenance served as sentinels that stood and shouted: Fall is coming; fall is coming!

And I would be fully remiss should I neglect the most delightful work-related outdoor endeavor from those days past. This one was cotton picking. Hot, tiring, difficult – but delightful just the same. We had our own family fields, but picking them was often a lonely affair, with perhaps only two of us dragging sacks and stuffing them with fluffy white. The one most entrenched in memory was shared by our little community church. We used the field to generate funds that were placed in the offering on one special day each fall we called Harvest Day. Both the cotton picking and Harvest Day were social gatherings much anticipated by all involved.

Practically all church members showed up for picking day. The able bodied snatched glowing fibers from fist-sized bolls; others cooked stew and made jugs of iced tea. Sweet, of course! And if you have ever crawled into a truck load of freshly picked cotton, you know the delight. It is a sensory journey like no other.

While the true essence of autumn did not then nor does now arrive in September, there was and is ample warning of its imminent appearance. And with it comes perhaps the most welcomed change known to the South. That is none other than the cessation of oppression handed out by summer's sinister grip. This begins to relinquish its hold in autumn. Life is quickened, refreshed. Outside is no longer the place to avoid; rather, it is the place that beckons. It is the place to be.

September is a reasonable time to enter training for the promises of autumn.

Good Dog: A Simple But Essential Ingredient

Everybody needs a good dog! I admit there is little or no objectivity present in that proclamation. It is a purely subjective viewpoint coming from one who can't imagine life minus a dog. But then some qualifying is in order. There may be physical or geographic limitations that preclude dog ownership. Such things are legitimate and best heeded. Those aside, however, I hold firm: Everybody needs a good dog.

As many of you, I have had exposure to a wide assortment of good dogs. Some were mine; others belonged to friends. Just the same, they were all good dogs. And my life is richer from having experienced them. Contrary to what may seem logical, I was always the learner rather than the teacher. It was the dogs who possessed the greater wisdom – perhaps in an odd canine fashion, but wisdom just the same.

I remember well those first two that were mine, chosen specifically for me. Beagles they were, Herman and Homer. I got them as pups when I was a pup, and they saw me through the first two years of college. Homer was the comedian. Always ready to explore anything that resembled fun, he was not the dedicated rabbit hunter I had hoped he would be. Oh, he would chase a rabbit, but he was also willing to leave a track completely to check out a terrapin or watch a squirrel scurry up an oak. He taught me how to see life as an adventure.

Herman, on the other hand, was fully dedicated to the task of rabbit hunting. He didn't know quit, and this led him to be held in high esteem among my hunting companions. Problem was, he never wanted to abandon the woods.

One afternoon late, Herman was off in the distance and refused to come when called. We had to leave for home, and there was no choice but to go without Herman. I laid my hunting jacket on the ground and headed in, concern for this little dog haunting me. The next morning I returned to the jacket and there was Herman, drawn there by my scent on the ragged coat. It was as if he knew I would come. He taught me trust.

There was Barlow, a cur that belonged to my friend Neal. Barlow was a squirrel dog, the best I have ever seen. He would hunt for anyone, but he was devoted to Neal. Barlow showed me what true loyalty was.

There was White. We rescued her from a road ditch, along with her sister Honey. We raised the two on a bottle and both became truly grand companions.

Once I was in a bitter episode with life's struggles. All seemed bleak; no end in despair could be seen. I walked into my back yard in search of any comfort I could find in the natural world and gazed upward. The gift White gave came subtly. I became aware of her presence and the gentle licking on one of my hands, hands that hung limp from a broken spirit. I looked down at her and patted her head. The look she gave was one of understanding, perhaps more understanding than I could grasp. It was as if she was telling me that all would be well. And it was – all was well in time. The despair, though real at the moment, was short lived, probably even ill entertained. Patience was the lesson learned.

And let's not forget unconditional love. Even when we don't

deserve it, dogs give it unconditionally. They love us in their own unique dog ways. We would do well to practice such.

A sad commentary is to see dogs disregarded and thrown away, left to an often merciless world. This should not be. No one or no thing should be treated in that manner. But it happens. Tragic, it is. Perhaps you should adopt one of the forgotten. It could change your life. For everybody needs a good dog.

That Perfect Day in the Squirrel Woods: Unexpected Gifts

Faint praise would be grossly inadequate. A mindless cliché would be wholly insufficient, irreverent. Most likely spoken with no depth of thought, that often heard "It could be worse" would be an affront. None of these; not for this day. This day was spectacular, its perfection melding with a lonesome fog that resisted the sun and gave naked oaks to the east a more foreboding appearance than normal. January; 48 degrees; sunrise; exhaled breaths puffing and pushing a gentle cloud into windless surroundings; no noise save the symphony of nature. Spectacular.

I sat alone, ideal for such activity. In pretense I was squirrel hunting, but I probably wasn't. Attire was basic, the type dress promoted by such a setting. The most significant piece was a tan game vest. It was the last my uncle bought and used extensively, but it remains functional. He was a simple man, asking nothing more in recreational tools than a cane pole and barely reliable bolt-action shotgun. He died in his early 80s almost 10 years back. I have had the vest since.

And then a sound, one that never fails to transform the present to some distant past. A pileated woodpecker. He first chattered and soon came bouncing by in that up-and-down flight pattern. He stopped on a tree and was immediately joined by two more of his kin. It is this bird I most associate with similar mornings as this in the squirrel woods with my dad. I was at first alarmed by that raucous call back then, but my dad assured me, explained what I was hearing. Can it possibly be that was more than 50 years ago? Alarm has since morphed into solace.

The rifle in my hands was a classic, a Marlin lever 39A .22. This basic platform has been in production going on 100 years now, and though the one I held had cosmetic changes, the model remains pretty much as it was at its introduction. I wanted one throughout childhood, but finances would not allow. That desire never faded, so I treated myself not too many years back. No buyer's remorse. The little rifle proved more than I had longed for since 1 was 12.

With the sun now forcing misty fingers through the fog and between bare limbs and around sturdy trunks of oaks that were waiting patiently for spring and new birth, a pair of wood ducks whistled by. A flock of geese honked from high overhead. A single-file string of does nibbled along, unaware of my presence. One suspected something and did that head-bobbing maneuver in my direction. She concluded, if indeed she did see me, that I was no threat. Her conclusion was correct. They pattered quietly on damp leaves and melted into a pine plantation.

And there were squirrels. One in an oak nearby, five or six bouncing around the treetops over there to the right. But actually taking one or more of these gradually became a matter of less import than I had envisioned while driving to the woods earlier. I was content to watch and think and find great refreshment in the moment.

I considered some words of Solomon. You know those from Ecclesiastes where he, a wealthy, powerful man possessing every material thing he could want and experiencing every perceived pleasure that could come to mind, laments, "Vanity of vanities," this

from the King James Version. The New International Version trans-
lates it "Meaningless! Meaningless!" Solomon goes on in this same
thought process to say, "What do people get for all the toil and anxious striving with which they labor under the sun?" – Ecclesiastes 2:
22 (NIV). Strong words demanding thought. I thought.

Here I was experiencing a prodigious supply of unexpected
gifts. None of them required "toil and anxious striving." They were
gifts. Foolish I would be not to recognize them as such and grasp
each for what it was, allow them individually and collectively to en-
rich and energize my life that, like the life of everybody else I know,
is filled with daily struggles and fatigue from the mundane. This
perfect day in the squirrel woods was running my cup over with
rich rewards.

Perhaps, either literally or figuratively, there is a tan game
vest in your closet. Perhaps there is a vintage .22 collecting dust in a
corner. You might consider dragging out these items from the past
and making them a part of the present and future. A perfect day
could be hidden in them.

Renew the Imagination;
Revisit the Dream

In the middle of confusion or darkness or sorrow or any combination of these and perhaps more, how can the imagination imagine or how can a dream be dreamed? No easy answers here. And no realistic way to categorize the above mentioned conditions. They vary with the individual; their degrees vacillate from mild to severe. But make no mistake; the conditions do exist. Life assures that. Confusion related to economic matters, darkness that permeates health issues, sorrow associated with loss. All are present at some point.

That recognition, though somewhat beneficial in dealing with such circumstances, still leaves behind the question of how. September could be a solution of sorts, a soothing balm of healing.

For instance, observe the first leaf that postures a hint of autumn. It will be available in September – probably on a sweet gum or black gum, maybe even a hickory. Its promise is grand, refreshing. Mississippi's heat has been unrelenting since June. It has worn and yet wears on frayed emotions that cry out for relief, hunger for change. That leaf speaks of hope, helping us in its quiet and unobtrusive way to imagine. That imagination may then lead to an absorption in the moment that takes away the sting of other surrounding realities. We can be made more resilient and better able to address those realities through this brief respite afforded by that single leaf, that gift of nature.

Feel the breeze. It will not be especially chilly in September, but it will hold some peculiar essence that has gone missing for months now. Imagine what that breeze meant during childhood. It surely must have had some impact on life, even if subliminal. It could allow the gentle recipient time to reach into the depths and extract strength to move forward.

Stop on a September afternoon and breathe deeply, listen intently. The aromas are of mown hay, pumpkins, fall gardens. The sounds are of rustling corn stalks, chirping insects, the drone of a distant farm implement, the ripple of a stream, the caw of a crow, the raspy chatter of a woodpecker. There may even be the high-school band at practice or the thud of shoulder pads on the gridiron just around the corner. Some keen reminders of youthful abandon and merriment. Some mental portraits of quiet and peace. All more than capable of generating sentiment that spreads its medicinal qualities on bruised spirits.

And consider the sky. It is distant and clear in September. Patchy clouds drift gracefully in an orb of azure. This space above tugs us upward, there where dreams originate. It then becomes almost impossible to ignore those dreams, some of which may have become dormant, stagnant, waiting only for such a moment as this to emerge from the dross of neglect. And once rekindled, these dreams may blossom with new vitality, sufficient to prompt us into making them a reality to meld with other perhaps less kind realities that have come without our welcome.

Perhaps this discourse has come full circle, bringing us back to that original question of how we can imagine and dream. Perhaps the question is more accurate when we ask how can we help but imagine and dream, particularly in those times of confusion, darkness, sorrow. September is the perfect time to allow that imagination to run free and consider possibilities, to permit ourselves to dream dreams that could shape life in days to come.

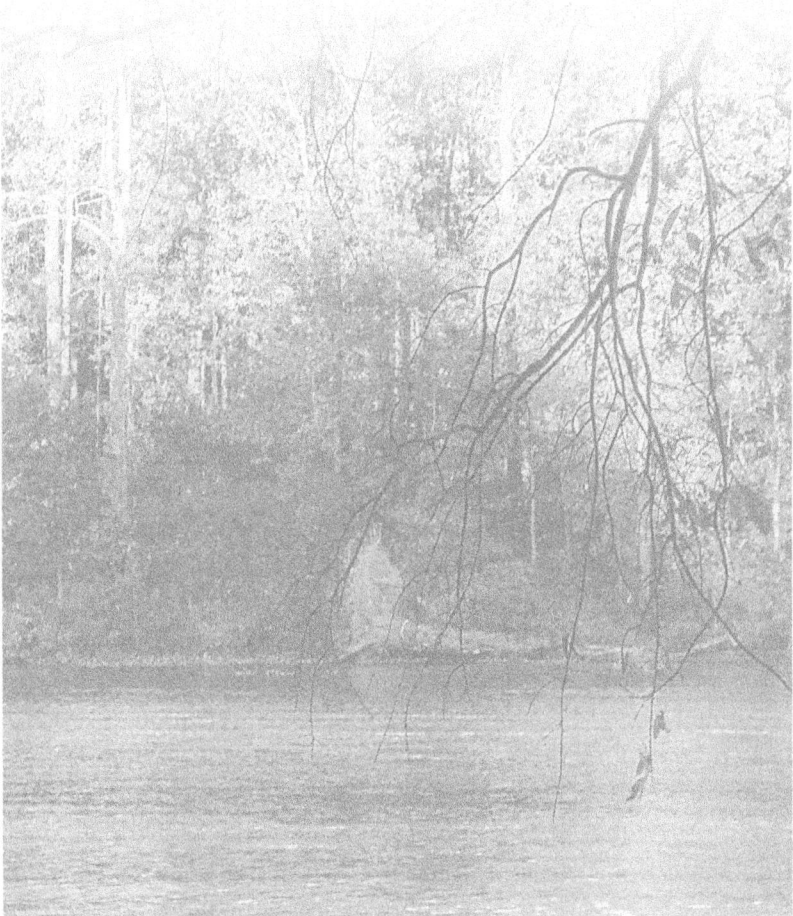

Actually Camping
at Hunting Camp

We toss the words hunting camp around with great abandon. And just the mention of those words paints a mental picture
of the location, even the smells and tastes and thrills associated
with it. This is a grand place, hunting camp.

But if we take the concept apart and open it to serious
scrutiny, we can argue that hunting camp may actually be missing
an ingredient found in the very words hunting camp. One definition of camp given by Webster is: "A place where tents, huts, bar-
racks, or other more or less temporary structures are put up...." The
emphasis, at least in this writing, is on temporary. Many hunting
camps are anything but temporary. Yes, a hut or shack or camp
house – whatever you choose to call it – is not permanent as is a
dwelling house. But neither is it temporary, unless, of course, it is a
camping trailer or such. To complete the idea of temporary, perhaps
we should look at the most time-proven form of temporary housing
known, an entity that has been in use for practically as long as humanity has existed. And that is none other than the tent.

There may be few among you readers who have the admit-
tedly sentimental proclivity to tents as I. Some would even see it as
some type warped sense of a misplaced search for pain. Not so. I do

not seek pain. But I do seek the primal rewards of actually camping in a tent. It, at least to me and thousands of others across the country, makes camp a camp. Whether in the High Country of the West or a quiet woodlot of central Mississippi, a tent defines camp. No, we here in Mississippi won't see the golden leaves of aspens or likely hear the gentle splat of snowflakes or the bugle of bull elk, but we can experience all a tent has to offer in the hills and hollows and bottomlands of the Magnolia State.

Why a tent? There are too many reasons to explore in this limited space. But let's take time to consider a few.

There is that magic smell and feel of a tent, particularly if you use a canvas structure. Nothing else compares. It has a texture and aroma that is distinct, something that once experienced will not be forgotten. And it speaks of the outdoors, of adventure, of emersion in nature. You are close to the world outside, separated by only the thickness of the material. That element of tent camping has a peculiar and most attractive allure.

And there are the aesthetics. A collection of off-white canvas tents is in the minds of some what a camp should look like. It is that ingredient in a hunting situation that beckons almost as much as the game pursued, that ingredient that calls you back almost as quickly as you leave. You look forward to the campsite. This anticipation is especially acute if such a camp is not something with which you are accustomed. It sets the mind free to wonder: Who in the past camped in this fashion; who is doing so now; where are there other tent camps set up; are these covered with snow?

And it sets you free to wander as well as wonder. A tent camp is mobile. Live on and hunt this piece of land today. Try another tomorrow or next week. Camp easily and quickly goes with you.

And there are the sounds heard only, or at least more fully, from a tent. Too often hunting camp can be filled with noise not unlike that of home or office, noise that most attempt to avoid while in camp. With technology being what it is, getting away from such noise is not always easy. More established camps may have TVs or stereos or computers and all manner of gadgetry that demands attention. All fine if that is what you want, but if you seek something else, less if you will, a tent can provide.

Inside those thin walls the monotonous and often discouraging TV news can be replaced by the yapping of distant coyotes. The thump of stereos can be replaced by the chirping of insects. The glare of computer screens can be replaced by the dim flicker of a campfire just outside. These are far more pleasing if you seek authenticity, if you long for a time of reflection and true rest. And that rest will often be accompanied by the soft flutter of tent walls in an autumn breeze or the gentle patter of raindrops on a cloudy evening. But the tent is built for this; it will endure them just fine and serve to serenade with a haunting lullaby.

And there is that coming alive of a new day that is more fully appreciated from a tent. Dew or droplets of water from last night's shower will patter on the roof. Crows will caw and scold. A squirrel will shake a limb. A deer may snort. Birds may sing. And in spring, a turkey may gobble with gusto and bravado from the next ridge over. These are the companions of tent camping, all worth the effort of going, even if no game is located that day.

Be assured, also, that pain does not figure into a properly-developed tent camp. Well-built tents are weather worthy; they keep out the rain and wind. There is a broad assortment of bedding available to keep the camper warm and cushioned from the ground. Safe, reliable heaters can be had. As can lanterns and cook stoves and folding tables and chairs. And we certainly must not overlook the Dutch oven when preparing a meal. These are old reliables and can produce camp food that demands second helpings.

So this hunting season, why not go camping? Really camping! Hunting camp will take on a new meaning from that point forward!

Country Wisdom and Predicting the Future

One distinct advantage to country living is the collection of small towns associated with the lifestyle. And I suppose I should add also the marvelous tales emanating from a great many of those so domiciled. Grand stories and small towns seem inseparable, for it is in these towns that folks gather. Enter any retail establishment and you are likely to find someone you know. And that someone will want to talk. So, please don't rush; take time to visit. Hurrying away could cause you to miss matters of significant import.

In just such a setting it was that I found myself on April 18th. I had stopped in at a store that handles practically everything from plumbing and electrical supplies to pocket knives and baseball caps. I walked in wearing knee high lace-up boots, a sloppy hat, faded jeans, green chamois shirt and carrying a wooden longbow. No one thought anything of it. I was there to buy a section of PVC, but fortunately not for plumbing. I was intent on fabricating a tube for the take-down Osage bow that would fit in my duffle for a trip to Africa. When I announced my purpose for being there, all ears turned in my direction. But soon my story grew dry and inconsequential, and the subject turned quickly to weather. A perfect topic, politics aside.

"The weather forecast says it's gonna be cold tomorrow," one customer noted. Tomorrow would be the 19th, but it was the 22nd that immediately became the focus.

"You know it will," the lady at the register added. "It thundered February 22nd and it is always cold in April around the same date it thunders in February. It will probably frost." Two days off is not so bad when making a long-range prediction with nothing more than the past as a radar.

"It won't frost now." Another customer entered the debate. "The bluebirds have already laid their eggs."

"Well, the eggs may freeze 'cause it's gonna be cold." There was now another individual opining in reference to this long-held belief. I had to agree with the prognostication of cold weather, for as long as my mother was cognizant and capable, she recorded any day in February when there was thunder. Seldom did the pattern prove false. And if you are wondering, yes, there was a touch of frost during that cold snap. All this banter set me to thinking of the many truths, perceived or otherwise, I had heard during my life in the country. And since most were somehow affiliated with nature, I concluded that these would fit in an outdoor column such as this is purported to be. Here are a few:

It's too cold to snow: I have heard this all my life in regards to Mississippi. But after I was the first time in snow with temperatures far below freezing, I began to question this. However, there is likely some element of truth when confined to the immediate area. We get our coldest weather when the sky is clear and heat is able to escape. Snow doesn't fall from a clear sky.

Stinging snakes bury up in the mud and wait for somebody like you boys to step on them: While likely believed by a scattering of folks, it was probably employed to keep errant barefoot boys from walking in the mud – and ultimately tracking assorted debris attached to the feet of those errant barefoot boys into the house.

I close with a few more upon which I will not expound:

A dream told before breakfast will come true.
If the wind spreads a chicken's tail feathers, it is going
to rain.
If you see lightning in the south, it will be dry weather.
It will soon rain when smoke from the chimney falls
to the ground.

True or false – these old country sayings? I don't know. But I do know that I will eat black-eyed peas and pork on New Year's Day! And like the words to that old song as these relate to my life in the country, I shall not be moved.

Memory Makers

All of us have memories, some cheerful and some perhaps glum. But regardless of the mood these evoke, they are there; they help make up who and what we are. And it is curious how these memories are triggered. Sight, sound, smell. Some external stimulus meets something there deep inside and brings recall.

While looking for a particular item beneath the stairs in our utility room recently, I came across a pair of boots. Ragged, worn and pretty much useless now, those old boots prompted a barrage of runaway emotions. The day I strolled into a local Western Auto and ordered them came fresh to my mind.

I was young, still in college – the 1960s. The proprietor knew me well from my frequent visits there to admire his rack of Browning A-5 shotguns. These were certainly beyond my budget, but I stopped and looked just the same. And the boots were out of my budget as well. Cost $40.00 or so if memory serves me correctly. But I asked the guy if I might pay for them in three installments. He agreed to order my size and let me pay them out as I could, this done on a handshake. The sun was shining brightly on that summer day. I retrieved the boots, paid in full, within three months, ample time to break them in before hunting season.

I picked up the boots there under the stairs and looked them over. Thoughts moved from that initial purchase to days afield. I took my first deer while wearing those boots, a somber but joyful memory. I recalled the many miles I put on them while trekking the bluffs west of Port Gibson and the river bottoms of the Pearl near home and the fallow fields of our farm in search of quail and rabbits. The boots even served as a lead once for an article I did for some hunting magazine. I remembered it: The prairie mud clung tenaciously to my old boots. Received some accolades for that piece.

As I stood there fondling those boots, I wondered once again why I had not discarded them. I set them out to do just that, but then thought more about such a drastic and terminal move. An epiphany emerged.

Perhaps usefulness is broader than we assume. The boots are not suitable for wear, but they have not lost their usefulness. They can no longer protect the feet and ankles; instead, they have morphed into something far more beneficial. They remind. They haunt. They allow the spirit to soar. I put them gently back beneath the stairs.

The same can be said for an old brown canvas hunting vest. I put it on occasionally but never wear it to the field. It is identical to the one my dad used; that's why I got it in the first place. And it smells the same. That smell is one of the outdoors, of trust, well-being, security. It no longer totes shotgun shells or squirrels or rabbits or quail. It totes memories, peace. Far more valuable in this duty it is than in the hunting venues.

My mom always hummed while she was preparing breakfast – a soft, melodious tune of some old hymn. Still does I'm sure, but I'm never there on such occasions these days. The sound wafted about the wood-frame house with no competition from technology, accompanied by the smell of home-cured bacon. The message received by waking ears and noses? All is well.

A hum may appear inconsequential, basically useless. That, however, is not true. Like those boots and vest, a hum can promote thought. It can transport and refresh and calm. It can be the perfect prescription in times when an antidote not found on the drug store shelves is badly needed. It is, like those other items, of great value. Far too valuable to cast aside.

Perhaps in troubled times we would all do well to look at our worn boots or tattered vests or listen to soft hums. We could be better for it.

Reflections and Projections

Depending upon where you are located, winter's grip could have taken hold. There could be snow on the ground, a blanket of white bringing gentleness to a rugged landscape. Or summer could be evident, the sun burning down with little hope of abating. Hunting seasons could be recently passed or ongoing or a few months in the future. Regardless of the conditions, however, this is a time of holidays, of celebration, of planning for a new year. And it is a time for reflection.

Just this morning I was contemplating the future and recalling the past. These ramblings focused not exclusively on hunting, but that endeavor occupied a large part of the mental journey. As this is being written, the fall hunting seasons are only weeks away. That realization brought to mind experiences from the past, particularly those only recently concluded with the spring turkey season. It was one of great import.

I had been trying for two years to take a big gobbler while using a stone-tipped arrow. That first season was of no consequence, for the turkeys didn't frequent my property with any regularity; the times I was there they were on land to which I had no access. The second season was much more promising. One afternoon the gobbler obliged by coming to my call, and from the confines of a pop-up blind I watched him strut and gobble and drum for half an hour

159

or more on the edge of a clover field; however, the distance was just too great. I drew the little Osage bow several times, but I opted to relax the string rather than release it.

This past spring the shot came. Along that same clover field from that same pop-up blind, I encountered that same gobbler. He worked perfectly into my calling and presented the shot I wanted at a distance that was fully acceptable. The Osage bent with ease and the arrow left in flawless fashion, a stone point tipping the shaft. I missed! Two inches to the left. Disappointed? Somewhat. But the turkey is still there; I saw him this past week. And I will see him as I sit and wait for deer on the property this December and January.

There was a big doe in October prior to the turkey. The arrow, cast from an Osage/bamboo rig, was true. I ate the last of that very fine venison just yesterday. And the big ten point of this past December? I recalled him. He followed other deer – does, yearlings, small bucks – into a tiny field in late afternoon. Only seconds from my release of an arrow on a broadside target, the buck nudged a doe. She bolted with the buck in pursuit. I watched in amazement and gratitude as the buck chased the doe, all the while grunting and wheezing. It was glorious, and that buck is still there on the same property that contains the turkey.

The future then came to mind. What will I do? What resolutions will I make?

I resolved a bit early for a New Year's resolution perhaps, to hunt that buck this December and that turkey this upcoming April. Whether I take either is of little concern, for I resolved many years ago to cherish the experience and be fully grateful for the opportunities that God gave to refresh myself in His creation. I resolved to be out there, bow in hand, whenever possible, awed by an autumn color spectacle or a dusting of snow or an explosion of spring blossoms.

I also resolved years back to recognize this season we are now in as a special treasure, a time to spend with family in giving thanks, in celebrating the gift of love. And my holiday wish for you is that you have the opportunity to do likewise. This truly is a time for reflections and projections.

Listening to and in
a January Woodlot

January is not likely the first choice as a perfect time for communing with the natural world. True, there is some incredible hunting afforded during this month, but not everyone is a hunter. And there are some pleasant days scattered about, days that are brisk but sunny and inviting. There are, however, and perhaps more often than not, those days of dreary nothingness. This is deep winter in the South. Glum skies can cause an otherwise cheerful countenance to be downcast. Biting cold can prompt exposed cheeks and noses and fingers to seek the refuge of warmth. January can be disagreeable.

But it can also be alluring. Even its austerity is capable of touching the very core of one's being and motivating that one to look at life deeply, to be reflective and introspective. We all need these exercises. They help us more fully realize who and what we really are. They allow us, even encourage us, to escape from the superficial that so often permeates the everyday and trek quietly into depths that are the essence of life.

While I don't recall the specifics, it was on such a day and in such a setting that a character from the first book in my "Wagon Road Trilogy" series made his first appearance in my mind (this from "Summer Lightning Distant Thunder"). Simon Keats strode into my consciousness on a January afternoon in a Mississippi woodlot and began talking. In his conversation with Jackson (Sun) Bain, the leading male character, Simon responds with wisdom that belies his country lifestyle. Sun notes:

"You seem to talk a great deal about this Good Lord as you call Him." There was a blatant air of sarcasm in Sun's voice as he spoke these words and gestured toward the heavens, heavens that were gloriously decorated this evening by the one to whom Sun referred with such a cavalier manner. "Are you some religious fanatic or something?"

"Ain't religious a'tall, most folks would say. Ain't been to church reg'lar since I come to the frontier. 'Course, they ain't many churches on the frontier to go to no how. Guess my church is mostly the trees and fields and rivers. Guess I'm part of the same congregation as the critters out here. But that don't mean I ain't in contact with the Almighty. Me and him talk reg'lar....And when the Good Lord is finished with me in this world, I know where I'm a goin'. Do you?"

"I never had much use for all that. I am fully acquainted with the church; my parents saw to that. And I suppose I believe in God. But this talking with God and knowing what awaits at the end of this life is something I don't think we can do. I believe God gave us intelligence and resourcefulness and expects us to use both as we live. I just can't see Him being available to talk with and such things."

"Sorry to hear that. But me, I talk to Him every day. Ain't plannin' to stop no time soon."

"And I guess you are going to tell me now that He answers you when you talk."

"Well, not so much when I talk, but when I listen He shorely does answer. Now ain't no words I can acc'lly hear. More like this little whisper, this little tuggin' in my heart. Yup, ain't no doubt it's God alright."

Simon was right. It is the listening and not the talking that is of most importance. January is here and a January woodlot is the perfect place to sit and listen. Perhaps we all should do this more often.

Africa:
A Land of Intrigue
Introduction

For as long as I can remember, the simple mention of
Africa sent my imagination soaring. I had seen the old Tarzan
movies and read adventures of many who spent time on that mysterious continent. And while I obviously suffered from an abundance
of erroneous information, I knew that I must see this strange and
magical place. Little did I realize then that such seeing would demand more than a lifetime. One life is hardly adequate to absorb
even a miniscule sampling of that great land. But back then, when I
was a child, I considered nothing more than the fact that I wanted
to go.

June 30, 2002, I found myself boarding a jet bound for At-
lanta, Cape Town and then on to Johannesburg. I was 54; my
dream had required almost half a century to materialize. That, however, was of no consequence. I was finally going to see Africa.

The day was typical for that time of year here in Mississippi – hot, steamy. But I had been taught and told that winter
would be in full swing in the Southern Hemisphere. That concept
was difficult to grasp; winter comes in December, not July! However, some 20-plus hours later I stepped on wobbly legs from the

big aircraft and into a grand display of azure from a cloudless sky and temperatures that coaxed me to pull a jacket from my duffle. Africa! I was here. The dream was alive. And like that dream, I, too, was alive, perhaps as much so as ever I had been.

The intent of this trip was safari, that mystical adventure hunters have sought for generations. The word conjures up visions of roaring lions, trumpeting elephants, suspect and intimidating Cape buffalo, and maybe even native drums in the distance on a quiet evening. But none of those animals were on my list of hoped-for encounters. And as I soon learned, no menacing messages would be riding the thuds of drums here. To the contrary; all was comfortably civilized. This was South Africa, a well-established country boasting thriving cities and commerce and well-kept farms and ranches. Lions and elephants and buffalo live here, but none would be present on the concessions we would visit.

We would pursue what is commonly known as plains game, a healthy, extensive gathering of horned beasts that roam in untold numbers across this almost endless landscape. And while their names are strange, their appearance can be quite familiar to anyone who has watched nature programs on TV: gemsbok, kudu, impala, blesbok, steenbuck, zebra, warthog, waterbuck, springbuck, blue wildebeest, black wildebeest. The list goes on to include 40 or so indigenous species.

And what of the condition surrounding all these and more? Healthy, secure; the future is bright. While some were once considered endangered, that designation has basically been rectified. Even the leopard is present in large numbers now. There is little talk of endangered, contrary to the belief of some individuals who are not fully schooled in the reality of what has been done and is being done. Game animals hold a peculiar slot of respect and care here. They are valuable and as such are protected through solid and on-going management. A safari is anything but a one-hunter endeavor; it is a parade of various personnel, including a PH (Professional

Hunter), trackers, rangers, and other government representatives. All keep a keen eye out to ensure everything is done with proper protocol. Absolutely no waste; absolutely no infraction of game laws. Everything is as it should be.

Hunting, like the game, is also respected. Subsistence hunting is a centuries-old practice. And beginning in the early 1900s, safari hunting entered the picture as a viable tool, both in herd management and economic impact. A great deal of business in this country revolves around safari. I mentioned waste in the paragraph above. There is none. Every scrap of every animal is put to use by those who need it. I was amused at this as native peoples came to collect all that was available. The meat was an important source of protein, and I was grateful to have the opportunity to supply this in the process of living out my long-held dream. It was the revelation of life providing life, of nature giving from a bountiful supply. It was sobering, reverent.

And here I was in Africa, a land of intrigue. I was to learn more than I ever imagined I would; I was to experience more than my former dreams held. I was off on safari, my first. Even at this beginning, I had already concluded it would not be my last.

Blesbok: My First Animal of Africa

The morning was chilly. Frost covered sage and browned grasses as a surreal sunrise chased darkness from ancient hills and plains. Only yesterday had I disembarked from a jet on which I had sat for more than 20 hours. But this day I was taking in the majesty of early morning in a land ripe with history. We were hunting blesbok.

Blesbok are curious creatures, odd looking, to be sure, but handsome. Mature rams feature a reddish coat with lighter belly. The head hosts a pronounced white blaze, above which are ringed horns that grow thick at the bases and spike into ivory tips. Quite impressive, these animals.

The property belonged to Deon, my PH. It covered 7,000 acres of rocky outcroppings; grass and brush-covered hillsides; and low, fertile strips along diminutive streams that were more often than not only trickles. Formerly a cattle operation that dated back to the late 1800s, the ranch stood abandoned after the last children of the owner grew up and moved to Johannesburg or Port Elizabeth or Cape Town and became accountants or attorneys or medical professionals and their parents died. Ragged but ornate markers with a distinct German flavor told the story in an unattended grave yard, its fence now rusted. Deon determined to coax it all back into a better state of repair. He had begun work on the big rock dwelling, with the intentions of transforming it into a lodge that would house safari clients. That work was on hold as he gave himself to several weeks of hunters from France, Germany, and the United States.

The crisp air had prompted me to pull on a heavy sweater as we left the truck that morning, but an hour or so into the hunt and the exertion expended to climb those rough hillsides and koppies begged removal of said sweater. We stopped and sat, my rifle leaning against a rock and the sweater stowed in my pack. The chill that earlier had produced a gentle fog from each exhaled breath was now a memory, this replaced by the splendor of a bright African winter day and 60-degree temperatures. A soft breeze immediately dried the perspiration and quickened our spirits.

Then we saw blesbok, a band of nine rams. They first moved into a grassy spot outside the brush and just as quickly vanished in an uphill direction. My heart raced. Here I was, after all those years, actually in the middle of African game, and the game I had just seen was magnificent. I could ask for nothing more. A plan was then laid out. We would move straight up from where we were and attempt to stay downwind of the blesbok. Perhaps we could circumvent the rams and find them in another opening on the opposite side of the hill. We had gone only a short distance when we saw an eland bull, a relatively young specimen, loping gracefully along to avoid any additional interference we had created. The blesbok were not in sight.

But then we saw them again, first one and another and another, creeping from the brush into the grass. Deon was immediately behind his binocular, attempting to sort out the rams and isolate the most mature male of the group. "That one," he whispered as he nodded to the fifth in line. "Wait for him to get clear of the others." Deon set the shooting sticks up for me and stepped back quietly to allow full access to this traditional African shooting system. The shooting sticks, simply three small peeled poles lashed together to form a tripod, afford a steady rest and are to be expected and employed on all African hunts. My .300 fell into the notch with the integrity of concrete. We waited.

How long we stood there at maybe 75 yards from the rams, I am not sure. But in whispered fashion we discussed the animals, Deon always careful to verify that I had the right ram in view.

"Take your shot when he clears," Deon advised, and almost as if on some predetermined schedule, the ram I was after extracted himself from the others and stood statue-like broadside and at full alert. The .300 added its blast to the sounds of bird call and wind through the brush. The ram dropped where he stood, his comrades never hesitating to bound away.

"Good shooting," Deon said as he offered me a hearty handshake and then stepped aside to allow me to go to the ram and pay my respect. Deon was far too much the gentleman to rush in with boisterous hyperbole. He understood the emotions of the hunter, for he, too, is a hunter.

As I sat beside the blesbok and admired his muscular frame and battle scars, I hardly noticed Deon's soft approach. Eventually our eyes met and we each smiled. "When you are ready we will get him down the hill a little and go get the truck," he told me in a soft voice that belied his frame. "But don't rush yourself; we have plenty of time." I said one more prayer of thanksgiving and we began moving the ram. This long-anticipated safari could not have had a more perfect beginning.

Gemsbok: A Last-Day Serendipity

Long before I was able to take a safari, I had envisioned what I most wanted to hunt. The Big Five – lion, leopard, Cape buffalo, elephant, rhino – were quickly discounted as possibilities. Fees, time, and logistics were far too prodigious. But no matter; there is a bounty of other grand and impressive species that demand fewer days and less cash outlay. Among these are the gemsbok and kudu, incredible animals that fairly shout "Africa" with each appearance. But, they are difficult to hunt. Secretive, cautious – they will sulk away into brush or rush to the next province in hoof-pounding haste if they detect an intruder's presence. And here it was the last day, and I still had no gemsbok or kudu. I would leave for Johannesburg early the next morning.

"Are you willing to hunt hard and give it a full-day's effort tomorrow?" Deon had asked me the evening before while seated around the ubiquitous African campfire. I answered in the affirmative even though we had been doing for eight days prior exactly what he asked of me again. Both of us were fatigued and dreading a 14-hour drive to the airport. A day of rest to prepare for such an arduous task would be welcome, but we were there to hunt every minute we had available. We could rest later!

Sunrise was glorious, stretching orange fingers of light to creep through rock crevices and around acacia trees and thornbush and across expansive plains in the distance. We lay atop a ridge and glassed gemsbok in the valley below. Too far to even consider a shot. "They are tough animals," Deon allowed as we studied them with wonder and chilling excitement.

Gemsbok are one of Africa's most handsome specimens. They are muscular and big-shouldered and wear a tawny coat with a darker longitudinal stripe running end to end lower on the body. The tail is full length and tufted like that of a domestic cow, and the face is decorated with a blaze and blends of that tawny and dark. But the horns are the crowing jewel. These can be three-feet long or more, are basically straight up from the head and end in menacing points capable of inflicting serious or fatal blows.

And gemsbok use those horns for exactly that purpose. Many documented accounts have arisen where gemsbok killed lions. "And do not approach a downed gemsbok until you are sure of the situation," Deon had told me several times. "They are quite dangerous." I took him at his word. We continued to watch and try to develop a plan that would cut 100 yards or more from the distance. Nothing seemed viable.

But the herd began to move. It looked as if they would go over the next ridge, on the back side of which was another valley. Perhaps this was what we needed. We gathered our gear, backed off the escarpment out of sight and attempted to hurry as best we could to skirt the edges and get to the next valley. Perhaps an hour of ankle-twisting, lung-burning exertion was employed before we accomplished this maneuver, but we eventually found ourselves in what we hoped would be a profitable position. We tucked in tightly in the only cover we could find, a solitary thornbush with low-hanging limbs. The gemsbok herd crested the hill and began a determined trek downward. Deon busied himself with the spotting scope and binocular while I set up short cross sticks on which to rest the rifle.

"Three good bulls in that herd," he whispered. A curious

thing about gemsbok is that both cows and bulls have horns. And the females are equally as skilled as the males at using these formidable weapons for defense. In fact, cows often possess longer horns than bulls, and they are legal game. Some of the leading contenders in trophy quality and the record books are cows. However, we had agreed to take only males of all species, so any long-horned female gemsbok would be immediately disregarded as a target animal. Deon continued his scrutiny.

Then suddenly we found ourselves inundated by gemsbok. They had held hard the course set and now were passing by precariously close. What often is a long shot was transformed into one quite close. The leading edge of the herd was no more than 50 yards out, curious cows jerking their heads and shying away from the phantasmagoric figures beneath the bush. Things didn't look particularly promising for a while, but the herd kept moving about and drifting by our station. Then the best bull. "That's him; third in that line coming into view. Be careful with the shot and make sure nothing is behind him. Take him when you can." Deon's words were whispered and held a sense of urgency. We had this one chance before the entire herd became a fleeing and distant memory.

Crosshairs quickly settled on that perfect spot as the big bull moved free of comrades. That eerie morning calm was disturbed by a sharp crack from the rifle. The bull ran a short circle and crumpled. A dust cloud was all that remained of the others. A handshake from Deon said he approved of my handling of this situation, and I eased away from him toward a hard-earned gemsbok bull.

Kneeling beside the bull, I absorbed the wonderment of this moment. An African sun was now spangling the countryside with spots of bright light. A gentle wind rolled from south to north. Birds, their variety and numbers in titanic proportion, again began singing and calling and chirping in every imaginable intonation. It was a glorious day, and I had my gemsbok. Whether or not the kudu came later was of little consequence. I removed my hat and gave thanks.

Kudu: Grey Ghost of the Thornbush

Kudu appropriately earned their title: Grey Ghost. These spectacular animals are basically grey, with white stripes running top to belly along their bodies from nose to tail. A bright chevron decorates their faces, which are framed by outsized ears and bold eyes.

And those horns! They are a work in beauty and symmetry. Huge at the bases and tapering to ivory tips, these make two full spirals and perhaps begin a third on mature bulls. The double helix they are called. The fortunate hunter can stand behind a bull and look through the curls to the animal's eye. About the size of wapiti (American elk), kudu are perhaps the most prized specimen among plains game.

Grey ghost? Absolutely. They are creatures of brush, and they can be standing in an open spot of sunlight one second and be nothing more than a brief recall the next. They seem simply to melt. To drift away on the breeze like smoke, an apparition. Phantoms one might say. But, they are real. They are present in ample supply. They are just ghostlike and more than challenging to hunt. Thus the propensity of African hunters to pursue them. But be prepared if you choose to do so. You may leave the Continent minus your most-wanted animal – as I was about to do unless I had excessively good fortune the last half of this last day.

Deon and I had hunted kudu religiously three days at this point. We had tried spot and stalk, walking the bush in hopes of dislodging a bull that might afford a shot, and we had sat quietly on a koppie for hours with binocular and spotting scope. One afternoon we even employed a common tactic used by deer hunters, that of sitting near a green field and waiting for something to show. The field was alfalfa; mountains and heavy brush outlined it. A hundred or so guinea fowl and three tiny duikers were all that came. Combining each effort, we had seen only a scattering of cows and one small bull. Now we were watching the clock tick down to the end.

Time had come on that last day for us to begin making our way back to the ranch house where we were staying. A declining sun had already begun to cast menacing shadows across an inherently haunting landscape, and the bush was best left behind in favor of a substantial dwelling. The truck, commonly called the hunting car in Africa, bounced and groaned across rocks and sage in what was termed a ranch road, a battered and weather-worn two-track at best. There was one spot where the road ran through a virtually dry stream bed, and as Deon did his best to negotiate the obstacle with as much comfort as possible, it happened.

I was throwing glum glances upstream from my left-side passenger seat, while Deon ground gears and toyed with the four-wheel-drive mechanism, his eyes averted from anything save a safe passage over this near impassable clutter of rocks. And there, 400 yards away was the unmistakable sign of the grey ghost – a terrific and colossal double helix towering from the brush. "There is a kudu!" was my immediate response, and as quickly as I said it I found myself approaching embarrassment for being so foolish and eager at such an unlikely proclamation. Why would we see one now when we had seen no such bull before? The prospects were most unlikely.

But Deon confirmed after my bold shout had time to sink in. "Magnificent bull!" was his exclamation. As if programmed to do so, Deon shut the truck down and rolled from the door, his feet barely hitting the ground before he grabbed the shooting sticks and left in a run uphill from the stream. "Get your rifle," he shouted. I followed dutifully, my breath already coming in short gasps from the excitement even before we made a 300-yard dash up a steep hillside. He had seen something I missed – the bull and three cows tearing from the brush and heading uphill toward mountain cover.

Panting and trembling, I caught Deon just as he planted the sticks and rolled to one side to afford me access. "Take the shot; take the shot." He then slumped to his knees breathless and coaxed his binocular to his eyes with shaking hands. The bull slowed his long-legged gallop and my rifle rumbled. A jet of flame danced from the muzzle in the late-afternoon dimness. The bull was down; his trio of cows made haste to overtop the nearby peek. Deon slapped my back with more glee than I had yet seen in his business-like demeanor. He even put his arm around my shoulders and squeezed. I reciprocated, and I do believe I saw tears in his eyes. I know I had them in mine. We crossed a low sheep fence (this was a sheep ranch of more than 100,000 acres) and went to the bull. I had no words. I was able simply to sit by the fallen monarch and stroke those incredible horns. Deon was quiet and respectful.

Perhaps it is the hunter only who manages a solid grasp on the emotions of such a moment. And then again, it could be that not all hunters do so. I cringe when I see the high fives and foolish antics that have come to permeate the video market related to hunting. I shed a tear when I see some magnificent creature's antlers or horns jerked about in haste in what appears to be some misplaced effort at hyperbolic conquest. The essence of hunting is lost in such, and it is a grievous thing to me. Gratitude and respect, and even a deep element of sadness, should be the overriding forces rather than senseless gyrations. But then I am old school. Still, I choose to embrace the sentiments that come to me from deep within. Quiet respect tops that list.

After ample time in that mode, Deon suggested we go back

and get the truck and locate the trackers who had been riding with us earlier. We would need them and the vehicle to retrieve this massive bull. But that would take time, for the truck would have to be worked back across the stream and driven on a circuitous route to get to a gate and another ranch road. "When you are ready we will go," Deon said softly. "It is getting dark." It seemed that my kudu adventure was over. As it turned out, however, there was quite a bit more remaining.

"I'd like to stay here with the bull," I opined. Deon looked at me askance. It is not the PH's fashion to leave a hunter alone. But I insisted. It seemed only proper to stay beside this animal until he was safely in the truck and away from a multitude of night-time scavengers that might do harm to his absolute perfection in form and beauty and grace. The bull deserved nothing less. Deon agreed with some degree of reticence. He left me in a fast walk back down the mountain. It was then that a new adventure began.

Once Deon was gone and I was fully alone with the bull, night swallowed any semblance of day and the world came alive with uncommon sights and sounds. The sky danced and rejoiced with a celebration of the Creator. Odd, curious calls and moans reverberated about the hills and thornbush. I trembled; whether in fear of the unknown or in awe of the majesty is not certain. But I trembled. And I shuddered at the night chill that engulfed the air with a vengeance that was missing while a bright African sun held that air captive. No truck. I waited.

With that wait now approaching an hour, the night was full grown. If anything, it was more spectacular and menacing than it had been when light first gave way to darkness. The chill increased; the sounds became more ominous. I stroked the thick, rich coat of the bull and once again offered him my apology and gratitude. It was then that I looked up and studied the Southern Cross. I brushed the Milky Way, more pronounced and closer than I had ever seen it, with my hand. It was a spiritual experience and revelation that accentuated my awareness that God had made it all and had afforded me the privilege of being here, of absorbing His work. Again I shed tears and without reservation voiced a repeated two-word prayer: "Thank You; thank You; thank You…."

I was to learn later that Deon and the trackers had high-centered the truck on a rock and had great difficulty extracting it. Thus, the tardiness of their return.

But I eventually saw truck light, bouncing and swirling and twisting through the rocks toward my station. The kudu adventure was now over, and I was better for it. More refreshed; more revived. Indeed, all was well.

Africa Revisited

Limpopo Province, South Africa. Bushveld. Land of the acacia and baobab and wait-a-bit thorns. A place time has neglected, where bird call serves as alarm clock, where the human intruder can lie awake nights as baboons scold from their koppie and treetop dwellings at a leopard beneath. A place where that same human can brush the Milky Way with feeble fingertips while a campfire performs its perfect ballet, can see the Southern Cross vividly suspended in lucid skies.

The province derives its name from that river bearing the same: Limpopo. It forms a boundary between Botswana and South Africa. Zimbabwe and Mozambique are not far to the north – at least not far in African terms. It was here, in this land of protracted and monstrously perplexing mystery, I concluded years back that experiences are the finest form of wealth. I was now again inextricably bound by its intoxicating marvels.

We first spotted the nyala bull from our truck while changing locations on the concession. Red dust boiled from a ragged ranch road as we stopped to allow my PH, Louis Steenkamp, an opportunity for closer scrutiny through his binocular. Petrus, the tracker, sat quietly as Louis whispered instructions in Afrikaans to his brother Marinus at the wheel. I determined from the animated gestures that a viable chance for stalking was available.

"Do you want to try for this one?" Louis quizzed me in that fluid and beautiful South African accent. My response demanded no words, for evidence in the affirmative was given by a hasty gathering of quiver and bow. Simultaneously, three of us stepped from the truck and onto African soil. I fell in line behind Louis and Petrus. What at that moment could possibly become a quick end to the hunt eventually morphed into a series of events that were filled with discouragement and elation.

The evening before, several of us sat around a fire and talked hunting. Nyala became the centerpiece of that conversation, and Marinus coaxed us toward wonderment with his review of a Zulu legend regarding this grand animal.

According to that legend, all the spiral horns became involved in an argument, this focused on which among the various species was the most beautiful. Each would opine in expected fashion: "We are," so said the eland. "No, it is the kudu," a member of that fraternity added. "Impossible," noted the bongo. "We are the most striking of them all." And so it went. With no solution reached, the animals petitioned God to come down and settle the matter.

God obliged, and arranged all the spiral horns into a side-by-side line, along which He walked back and forth, admiring each individual. It is said that God finally stopped in front of the nyala, nestled the bull's face and head gently in His hands and proclaimed, "You are the most beautiful." The place just below the eyes where God's thumbs rested became that glorious white chevron. And where His fingertips touched along the jaw lines became those white spots. I could offer no credible argument with this tale, for only God could create such a grand and handsome creature as the nyala.

And on the afternoon prior to this fireside enlightenment, serendipity took place on another concession. We were on an errand to retrieve a huge warthog taken an hour earlier, when an aging tracker stopped and motioned to the ground. The spoor to which he referred was all but invisible, that is until he pointed it out. Louis interpreted. It was leopard dung that revealed the cat had been feeding on kudu. Evidence was ample, this supported by multiple pictures of two outsized leopards on game cameras.

That evening, after the discovery of leopard spoor and the sharing of marvelous tales from the African bush, I went to the tent and drifted off to sleep with hopes of hearing guttural grunts of this most intriguing of all felines. Being separated from a leopard by only a canvas wall is the stuff of dreams.

We made profitable progress in our stalk toward the nyala. The wind was right and heavy brush afforded ample concealment. Slowly and deliberately, we continued. I nocked an arrow. But then, with no provocation other than his own whims, the bull moved – maybe 100 yards and to another acacia cluster, where he busied himself with more leaf munching. The process had to stop so that a new stalk could be planned.

And so it was. This one, however, ended as the one before it. Two more times it happened. The sun was now beginning to cast haunting shadows and a chill had returned to the African air. Day four was coming to a close. This nyala could be slipping away, as were the remaining hours of the hunt. But then a sudden change. With Petrus holding back in the brush, Louis and I found ourselves within 20 yards of the preoccupied bull. It was time for a shot.

Most hunters recognize fully a new arrival that shows up about this same time within the completion of a chosen goal. It is a sentiment apart from target panic or buck fever or whatever you opt to label it; it is something more. It is not the question of whether or not the shooter can make the shot. I was confident of that fact. The question is and was: "Do I want to do this?" Such a moment seems ill placed after so much practice and expense and travel and distance, but there it was. That ache, that uncertainty. Time comes to a halt and the hunter, at least this is true for me, finds himself or herself in a bubble of anticipatory grief, its rough edges not yet sanded smooth by exhilaration.

But that hunter must choose; in this case I must choose. I could draw and release the arrow or I could simply smile and walk away. There would be rewards in either selection. I do not recall when the decision became firm, but I do recall the sight picture and the anchor and the realization that I was about to deliver meat to those who needed it badly and I would in the future be afforded the distinct pleasure of looking at the fingerprints of God on my wall. No recall of the release, but the arrow, without notice, smacked solidly into that pocket just at the upper knuckle of the front leg, behind which lay the heart. There would be no need for a tracker.

As I approached the bull and made certain that the end had come with haste and certainty, Louis and Pietrus waited from some distance back. They gave me the freedom to experience this entire episode in any manner I elected. For they, too, are hunters; they have felt the sobering sadness mixed to perfection with elation. There would be no high fives or senseless jubilation, though there was quiet satisfaction more than evident. I removed my hat and knelt in a long prayer of thanksgiving. Once again God had blessed me, Africa had embraced me, and all was well with the world.

And I Close:

"I will lift up mine eyes unto the hills,
from whence cometh my help.
My help cometh from the Lord, which made
heaven and earth. He will not suffer thy foot to be moved:
he that keepth thee will not slumber."

Psalm 121: 1 – 3. (KJV)

-END-

Visit: www.tonykinton.com

www.ingramcontent.com/pod-product-compliance
Lightning Source LLC
Chambersburg PA
CBHW032106280326
41933CB00009B/767